Intrinsic
Motivation
at Work

Intrinsic Motivation at Work

What Really Drives EMPLOYEE ENGAGEMENT

Kenneth W. Thomas

BK

Berrett–Koehler Publishers, Inc.
San Francisco
a BK Business book

Berrett-Koehler Publishers, Inc.
235 Montgomery Street, Suite 650
San Francisco, CA 94104-2916
Tel: (415) 288-0260   Fax: (415) 362-2512   www.bkconnection.com

Ordering Information
Quantity sales. Special discounts are available on quantity purchases by corporations, associations, and others. For details, contact the "Special Sales Department" at the Berrett-Koehler address above.
Individual sales. Berrett-Koehler publications are available through most bookstores. They can also be ordered directly from Berrett-Koehler: Tel: (800) 929-2929; Fax: (802) 864-7626; www.bkconnection.com.
Orders for college textbook/course adoption use. Please contact Berrett-Koehler: Tel: (800) 929-2929; Fax: (802) 864-7626.
Orders by U.S. trade bookstores and wholesalers. Please contact Ingram Publisher Services: Tel: (800) 509-4887; Fax: (800) 838-1149; E-mail: customer.service@ingram publisherservices.com; or visit www.ingrampublisherservices.com/Ordering for details about electronic ordering.

Berrett-Koehler and the BK logo are registered trademarks of Berrett-Koehler Publishers, Inc.

Printed in the United States of America

Berrett-Koehler books are printed on long-lasting acid-free paper. When it is available, we choose paper that has been manufactured by environmentally responsible processes. These may include using trees grown in sustainable forests, incorporating recycled paper, minimizing chlorine in bleaching, or recycling the energy produced at the paper mill.

Library of Congress Cataloging-in-Publication Data
Thomas, Kenneth Wayne, 1943-
  Intrinsic motivation at work : what really drives employee engagement / Kenneth W. Thomas.—2nd ed.
     p. cm.
  ISBN 978-1-57675-567-9 (pbk. : alk. paper)
  1. Employee motivation. I. Title.
  HF5549.5.M63T456   2009
  658.3'14—dc22   2008055553

SECOND EDITION
14 13 12 11 10 09   10 9 8 7 6 5 4 3 2 1

Cover designer: Susan Malikowski/Autographix
Interior designer and composition: Beverly Butterfield, Girl of the West Productions
Copyeditor: PeopleSpeak
Indexer: Rachel Rice

To Gail and Sarah

CONTENTS

PART FOUR
Leading for Engagement

PREFACE

This book will give you crucial new insights and tools for motivating workers in today's organizations. Why do you need this book? Because today's jobs are dramatically different from those of only a generation ago—and require much more initiative, creativity, and judgment. Today's jobs have changed so much that employees require a different kind of motivation. Organizations have recognized that need in the last few years and have begun talking about "employee engagement." But that term remains fairly vague and only points in a general direction. This book will give you a much clearer understanding of what employee engagement is, what powers it, and what you can do to create it.

This book comes from more than twenty years of work on intrinsic motivation—the force that drives engagement. I have interviewed engaging leaders and their followers, developed a research measure of intrinsic rewards with my colleague Walt Tymon, conducted surveys in a number of organizations, delivered workshops, written some influential journal articles, and consulted with public- and private-sector organizations. I have also learned a great deal from colleagues at the New West Institute, a firm that has used our research instrument and the first edition of this book in all of its consulting. This second edition of *Intrinsic Motivation at Work* draws upon all those experiences to give you the knowledge and tools you'll need to lead for engagement.

This book is organized into four parts. Part 1 will show you what engagement looks like on the job. Basically, engaged workers actively *self-manage*. They commit to a meaningful purpose, apply their intelligence to choose how best to accomplish the purpose, monitor their activities to make sure they are doing them competently, check to make sure that they are actually making progress toward the purpose, and make adjustments as needed. This self-management, then, is the key way that workers add value in today's fast-paced, global, service-oriented economy.

In part 2, you will get a clear picture of the rewards that power this kind of engagement. Active self-management requires more than economic rewards. It is energized and sustained by *intrinsic* rewards—psychological rewards that workers get directly from their self-managed work. The four main intrinsic rewards are a sense of meaningfulness, a sense of choice, a sense of competence, and a sense of progress. As you'll see, these rewards not only energize and sustain self-management, they also have powerful effects on retention, development, innovation, and other key outcomes.

Workshops have shown us that it is easier to learn how to engage other people when you first learn how to monitor and manage your own intrinsic motivation. So part 3 will help you tune into your own intrinsic rewards, introduce you to the major building blocks for each intrinsic reward, and spell out actions that you can take to build those rewards for yourself.

Then part 4 will give you the tools you need to engage the people in your work team. You will learn how to determine the strengths of your team members' intrinsic rewards, and you will learn acts of leadership that enhance each intrinsic reward. These actions go beyond familiar principles of job enrichment to emphasize the kinds of conversations and celebrations that keep people actively engaged.

A comment on style: I have tried to write this book in a fairly informal way that connects with your experience, so I'll share a few of my own experiences and ask you to reflect on your own, especially in the later chapters. As I wrote these sections, I tried to imagine myself in a conversation with you where I could speak honestly about what I think you need to know and do to successfully engage yourself and others.

One final note: because a lot of drama is involved in the kinds of changes this book covers—in the speed and urgency with which work has changed, in the shift from command-and-control to self-management, and in the changing motivational needs and opportunities of the new work—I have used a running "Management Tale" at the beginning of each part of the book to capture this unfolding drama.

ACKNOWLEDGMENTS

I have had the good luck to work with people who felt passionately about intrinsic motivation. Betty Velthouse, now at the University of Michigan-Flint, first got me thinking about empowerment as a research topic when she was a PhD student at the University of Pittsburgh. Walt Tymon, now at Villanova University, became a long-term research partner and lifelong friend on this adventure. Together, Walt and I developed the research instrument, now titled the Work Engagement Profile, which provides much of the research evidence cited in this book. Erik Jansen, my colleague at the Naval Postgraduate School, helped me sort through the conceptual underbrush around this topic. It was also Erik who first suggested I write this book. I am deeply indebted to each of them for sharing ideas, enthusiasm, and support.

I am also indebted to Bruce Vincent and Steve deBree at the New West Institute, who recognized the practical value of the ideas in the first edition and have used the book, along with our research instrument, in all their applied work with organizations. We have learned much from each other, and many of their insights have been incorporated into this second edition.

I would also like to thank those research colleagues who generously shared their research findings with me so that they could be included in this second edition—especially Professor Jacques Forest of the Université du Québec à Montréal and the research team who designed the large study of Indian companies conducted jointly with Right Management and including Richard Smith and Villanova University professors Steven Stumpf, Walter Tymon, and Jonathan Doh.

I am also indebted to Berrett-Koehler's reviewers and the friends and colleagues who gave me helpful feedback on various drafts of this book—Walt and Erik again, as well as Barry Leskin, David Jamieson, Robert Mountain, James Kouzes, and Beverly Kaye. I have tried to incorporate them as best I could but remain responsible for any lapses that remain.

My wife and partner, Gail Fann Thomas, was a sounding board for many of these ideas. She also provided me with a clear model of intrinsic motivation—someone who cares passionately about doing work that makes a difference and benefits others.

I want to thank the staff at Berrett-Koehler—especially Publisher Steve Piersanti, who created a firm that truly lives the principles I wanted to write about, and Editorial Director Johanna Vondeling, who helped me focus the second edition on what would be most useful to leaders. I also thank the American Society for Training and Development (ASTD) for agreeing to copublish this book along with Berrett-Koehler.

KENNETH W. THOMAS
Monterey, California
April 2009

PART ONE

What Engagement Looks Like Today

$\mathcal{A}$ Management Tale . . .

IN EARLIER TIMES, the executives turned to their most trusted advisers—the engineers and the economists—and asked how workers should be managed.

"Rationally," they replied, for such was their training. "Workers are often emotional and must be controlled. We must give them simple tasks with many rules and watch closely to make sure they obey them."

"And will they obey?" asked the executives.

"Yes, for they are poor, and we will deny them money and work if they do not."

"Very well," said the executives, and their advisers happily designed detailed Rule books and Compensation Systems and built tall Hierarchies to administer them. This took time, but the world moved slowly then, and there was little competition, and so their organizations prospered.

As time passed, the workers gathered into unions to protect themselves from low wages and firings. They shared in the general prosperity and became more educated. As this came to pass, they began to petition the executives that their emotional needs might be better met. This frightened the advisers, who truly believed that emotion was the doorway to Chaos. But the executives bade them modify the rules to permit modest participation and job enrichment, and their organizations prospered.

But shortly thereafter, as these things are measured, the executives beheld Great Change. The world grew small, competitors abounded in all its realms, and buyers of their wares began to demand great Speed, Quality, and Customization. As their Hierarchies and Rule books began to fail them, the executives again turned to their advisers.

"How can we meet these demands?" they asked.

Their advisers, of course, answered, "Rationally," and fashioned the cost-cutting sword of Value-added. Wielding this sword, the executives made great slashes in their Hierarchies. They also gutted the Rule books, that workers might better innovate and meet customer needs.

When the cutting was done, the executives found that much had changed for their workers. There were no tall hierarchies to closely monitor and direct them nor detailed Rules to comply with. *What, the executives wondered, will ensure that workers act responsibly now?* In answer, they heard the voices of new management gurus who spoke of the need for *Employee Engagement.* "Workers must feel Passion for the work and derive Fulfillment from it." And the executives heard in this message an echo of their own energy for work. However, the gurus spoke with many voices, and it was not clear exactly what Engagement meant nor how it worked.

So the executives, as before, turned to their trusted advisers, the engineers and economists. "How can we Engage workers by managing for Passion and Fulfillment?" they asked.

"We cannot answer that question," replied the advisers, "for it is not rational."

■ ■ ■

Clearly, thought the executives, *Engagement is a different sort of concept and requires new thinking.* So the executives selected a consultant renowned for his wisdom and approached him with their question.

"Much has changed for our workers. Can you help us to Engage them in their new work?"

The Wise Consultant pondered for a while and said, "Perhaps we should begin by looking at what is involved in the new work—to see what it is that you wish them to be Engaged in and how you might recognize Engagement when it occurs."

1

How Work
Has Changed

I find that a lot of people hold old assumptions about work that no longer apply. So this first part of the book will help you understand how dramatically work has changed, the nature of today's work, and what engagement looks like in today's organizations.

It is hard to grasp how rapidly and dramatically the worker's role has changed in this country. Consider that we even use different words to describe workers now. Few organizations still use the word *subordinate* to describe workers. Even the word *employee* has given way to *associate* in many Fortune 100 organizations. These word changes are a surface sign of the deeper shift in workers' jobs.

In *The New American Workplace,* James O'Toole and Edward Lawler provide a detailed analysis of workplace changes over the last three decades.[1] Look at their data in figure 1. In the twenty-five years between 1977 and 2002, there were huge surges in the number of workers who reported that their work was meaningful, allowed them discretion, and made use of their abilities. In roughly the span of a single generation, then, there has been a sea change in the nature of work.

What happened?

Figure 1. **Work Changes in the United States**

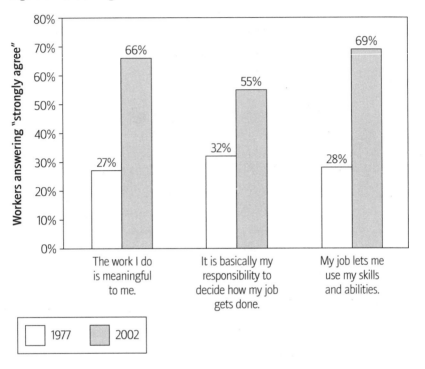

How Work Used to Be: The Compliance Era

From the beginning of the twentieth century until the 1970s, it was reasonably accurate to think of workers' roles in terms of compliance.[2] *Sound management* meant simplifying work tasks, producing thick rule books, and building tall hierarchies with close supervision to make sure that workers complied with the rules. This was command-and-control management in bureaucratic organizations. It was supported by the economics of the times: in a stable environment with heavy demand, the rules produced standardized products and services that met customer needs, and the simplified work meant lower pay and training costs for workers. Blue-ribbon companies of the time, including General Motors, General Electric, and American Telephone and Telegraph, exemplified this philosophy. And generations of managers and workers had time to get used to this reality.

The Last Three Decades

By the beginning of the twenty-first century, however, technology had changed the economic equation. Telecommunications created a truly global marketplace, with intense competition and the need for quicker responses. Customers demanded greater quality as well as customized products and services. Most organizations restructured to flatter, more agile designs that emphasized cross-functional teams and the free flow of information. Inside the organization, computers and automation reduced the number of low-skilled jobs and increased the need for worker judgment. Low-skilled jobs that could not be automated were often offshored to countries with lower wages. Computers provided workers access to the information that enabled decentralized decisions.

These conditions, as Warren Bennis had predicted years before, brought about the decline of bureaucracy.[3] The tall hierarchies and close supervision prevented workers from responding quickly to customer needs. The same was true of the detailed rules. One by one, Fortune 500 organizations announced large layoffs of middle managers and first-level supervisors, and CEOs condensed rule books down to a few guiding principles.

In most organizations, then, it is no longer a question of middle managers' *allowing* workers more choice and participation. Many levels of middle management and supervisory positions have been eliminated, and an organization needs its workers to take on many of their roles. Workers are often in different locations from their managers, making close supervision impractical. Instead of complying with detailed rules, workers are now asked to be proactive problem solvers. They must make adjustments, coordinate with other organizational players, innovate, and initiate changes. Workers are becoming strategic partners of top management, deciding the actions needed at the grassroots level to meet their organization's goals.

It is hard to draw precise boundaries around these changes. Some industries and job types come immediately to mind—"high tech" and "knowledge workers." But the new work is not confined to particular industries and job classifications. O'Toole and Lawler found examples of the new work in virtually every industry. The main differentiator seems to be business strategy. Organizations that choose to compete primarily as low-cost providers often continue to offer low-skilled, low-paying jobs that give workers little chance to exercise choice. Still, because of global competition and technological change, these organizations are now in the minority. Fewer and fewer organizations can afford to use people only for compliance.

In most of today's organizations, then, workers are required to be a greater source of problem-solving creativity and value-added than in previous years.[4] Keeping them motivated, using them well, and retaining them have become important to competitive advantage, or even a requirement for survival.[5] Jack Welch, former CEO of General Electric, put it this way: "I think any company ... has got to find a way to engage the mind of every single employee. . . . If you're not thinking all the time about making every person more valuable, you don't have a chance. What's the alternative? Wasted minds? Uninvolved people? A labor force that's angry or bored? That doesn't make sense."[6]

HOW WORK HAS CHANGED

Employee Engagement

In the last few years, organizations have adopted the phrase "employee engagement" to capture the kind of motivation required in today's workplace. It is the logical successor to earlier terms in the evolution of work. We began "enriching" workers' jobs in the 1970s.[7] Then we "empowered" workers in the 1980s and 1990s. And now that the work is more demanding and there is looser supervision, we need to make sure that workers are psychologically "engaged" in performing that work.

Unfortunately, "employee engagement" has been used in quite different ways by different writers, often without a specific definition.[8] A more specific and useful definition of engagement is the degree to which people actively self-manage in their work. (I'll cover this definition and the nature of self-management in more detail in chapter 3.)

The chapters in this book will give you a solid framework to help you understand and build employee engagement. Our focus will be on understanding how engagement shows up in a person's work, how you can recognize it, and how you can help to create it. The framework we use will build upon the key difference between old-school compliance jobs and most of today's jobs—the degree to which they provide *intrinsic* rewards.

So at this point, I'd better explain what I mean by "intrinsic rewards."

Intrinsic and Extrinsic Rewards

The downside of compliance-era work was that there was little in the work itself to keep workers motivated or satisfied. Consider the daily experience of a compliance-era job. Nearly everyone has had one—hopefully only for summer jobs or early in your career. Mine involved a white-collar job during summer breaks. There was some challenge in learning the detailed job rules at first, but that didn't take long. Then I settled into a boring routine, and much of my work behavior went on automatic pilot. If I had a question, I had to ask the supervisor. My mind wandered. I found myself watching the clock before breaks and toward the end of the day. I looked forward to anything that broke the monotony and started to invent mental games. I put unnecessary creativity into things that might give me satisfaction, like improving the quality of my printing. The only excitement involved a standing card game during the lunch break. I had to drag myself to work each morning but went because I needed the money.

When organizations wanted only compliance from workers, then, they bought it with money and other tangible benefits. In the language of motivation theory, these are *extrinsic* rewards. Extrinsic rewards don't come from the work itself; they are doled out by supervisors to ensure that work is done properly and that the rules are followed. They include compensation such as salaries, bonuses, commissions, perks, benefits, and cash awards.

Extrinsic rewards were an easy solution to motivation in the compliance era. They were *possible*. The tall hierarchies allowed managers to supervise workers closely so that they knew when rules were being followed and could give or withhold rewards accordingly. And the rewards were enough. Organizations only needed to buy rote behavior, not commitment and initiative. They didn't need to appeal to workers' passions or even enlist much of their intelligence. Finally, they were all management had to offer. With the simplified work and the constraining rules and procedures, few intrinsic rewards were possible.

As I mentioned, the new work requires a great deal of self-management by workers. Self-management, in turn, requires more initiative and commitment, which depend on deeper passions and satisfactions than extrinsic rewards can offer. Fortunately, the new work has the potential for much richer, *intrinsic* rewards. Intrinsic rewards come to workers directly from the work they do—satisfactions like pride of workmanship or the sense that they are really helping a customer.

I will spell out the intrinsic rewards that are possible in today's work in part 2 of this book. But to fully appreciate these intrinsic rewards, you need to understand two key aspects of the new work—purpose and self-management—for they are at the root of intrinsic motivation. We'll cover those topics in the next two chapters, beginning with purpose.

2

The Rediscovery
of Purpose

This chapter will help you understand the key role of purpose in today's work. As we'll see later, meaningful purposes are a foundation for worker engagement and self-management.

To begin, let's take a moment to consider the nature of work itself.

What Is Work, Anyway?

I invite you to take a moment to examine your own assumptions about work. Work is made up of *tasks*. What words or phrases come to mind when you try to define what a task is? If that is too general of a question, then pick a specific task your work team performs and think about how you would describe it to a new team member.

I've learned that there are two very different ways of answering that question. The first way reflects the traditional, activity-centered notion of work. It says that tasks are made up of *activities* (behaviors) that a worker needs to perform. So if you were explaining flight attendants' jobs, for example, you would mention activities such as giving safety instructions, serving meals and beverages, and distributing pillows. This is the way most of us were trained to think about workers' jobs. It is a notion of work that fit the compliance era very well, since compliance is about following behavioral directions.

The other way of answering the question involves a more purpose-centered view of work. It says that tasks are most fundamentally defined by the *purposes* they serve. If you were explaining flight attendants' jobs in a purpose-centered way, for example, you might say they are there to keep passengers safe, comfortable, and satisfied. Or you might mention the purposes as a way of explaining the task activities: giving safety demonstrations and enforcing FAA rules to promote safety, providing food and bedding for passenger comfort, and generally trying to keep passengers satisfied.

These purpose-centered answers reflect a fundamental insight about work tasks. Tasks are made up of more than the activities people perform. After all, those task activities only exist because someone chose them as a way of accomplishing a purpose. *Tasks, then, are sets of activities directed toward a purpose.* Betty Velthouse and I offered that insight in an article nineteen years ago, and I am still amazed at its importance.[1]

Rediscovering the role of purpose in work is key to understanding the new work and the motivation of today's workers. Without a clear notion of purpose, workers cannot make intelligent choices about work activities, and they are also deprived of a sense of the meaningfulness of their work. So, if you and others in your organization are still thinking about work in an activity-centered way, you'll have some rethinking to do.

Two Important Facts About Purposes

To help you understand the role of work purposes in engagement, you should know two basic points about purposes. First, work purposes generally involve events that are external to workers' jobs. That is, most work purposes involve outcomes that occur not to the worker, but to some customers (internal or external) in the worker's environment. There are some exceptions involving secondary tasks. For example, my task of cleaning off my desk is aimed at allowing me to better accomplish my main work purposes. But those main purposes involve meeting the needs of book publishers, readers, students, and research sponsors. Environmental needs like this create jobs in the first place. Importantly, meeting those needs—and having a positive impact on one's environment—is what gives the job its significance or meaningfulness.

The second point is that achieving work purposes is not totally under a worker's control and involves inevitable uncertainties. Because they are external to workers' jobs, task purposes depend not only upon workers' activities, but on outside events as well. For example, flight attendants' purpose of keeping passengers satisfied depends on passengers' moods, flight delays, turbulence, and the behavior of other passengers. Likewise, a forest ranger's success in keeping wildlife healthy depends on factors such as naturally occurring diseases, lightning-started forest fires, and the behavior of campers and hunters. The fact of these uncertainties provides much of the challenge and suspense involved in accomplishing work purposes—and produces much of the satisfaction in their accomplishment.

How Purpose Got Removed from Work

I'm going to give you some history and background here—to explain why purpose got removed from jobs for a long time, why it has suddenly and dramatically reemerged, and how purpose-centered leadership has become critical. This material helps leaders to reexamine some half-truths that were taught in management training in the not-too-distant past. (But if you are in a hurry, just jump ahead to the section called "Not All Purposes Are Equally Engaging" toward the end of this chapter.)

If purposes are fundamental parts of tasks, how did they get separated from traditional notions of work? The answer goes back to the early twentieth century when the industrial era was blooming. It was then that so-called scientific approaches to management began to develop, largely to meet the demands of the new phenomenon of mass production. The environment of the early twentieth century was considerably more stable and predictable than today's. That is, its uncertainties were more manageable for organizations. This meant that organizations could largely coordinate their tasks using two simple devices: centralized, hierarchical control and detailed rules and procedures.[2]

Let's start with centralized, hierarchical control. Because uncertainties were relatively manageable, managers could take on the responsibility for handling them. In effect, they walled workers off from the environment and its uncertainties. For decades, it was considered sound management to "buffer" workers from potentially disruptive environmental events and to "absorb" uncertainty on their behalf, and this language was reflected in the classic works on management.[3] Notice how paternalistic this language sounds today.[4] Managers essentially took over the decision making involved in handling uncertainties in order to achieve the task purpose. They became the "keepers of the purpose." Knowing about task purposes and their accomplishment became unnecessary for workers.

Without a knowledge of purpose, of course, workers could not make intelligent decisions about which task activities to perform or how to perform them. So management had to provide directions on what activities to perform and how to perform them—in the form of detailed rules and procedures. Worker judgment itself was seen as a source of uncertainty that needed to be controlled so these rules and procedures were also used to systematically eliminate choice from jobs. Industrial engineers determined the optimal sequence of activities needed in a worker's job and the optimal way of performing those activities—often down to individual arm movements. Frederick Winslow Taylor championed this "Scientific Management" approach to job design, which was also referred to as "time and motion" or "efficiency" work.[5] In short, work tasks came to be defined solely in terms of behavioral activities, and those activities were prescribed through detailed rules and procedures. Managers enforced compliance with those rules and procedures through close supervision and extrinsic rewards and punishments.

This treatment of workers seemed like the natural order of things during the industrial era. Machinery was celebrated as the great enabler of efficiency and productivity. Engineers became influential voices in organizations, and organizations themselves came to be viewed as machines. Managers tried to run their organizations like machines—rationally, predictably, impersonally, and efficiently. Their emphasis on centralized control and elaborate rules came to be called "machine bureaucracy." It was easy, by extension, to think of workers as imperfect pieces, or cogs, within the organizational machinery. The classic Charlie Chaplin film *Modern Times* provides a memorable caricature of this assumption.

Why Purpose Is Back at Work

Bureaucratic principles about management were so ingrained that it took a great deal of research in the second half of the twentieth century to show that there were significant exceptions. Organizations facing uncertain technologies and environments required less bureaucratic forms of organization.[6] But now, at the beginning of the twenty-first century, these "exceptions" have become the rule. The environment that was so stable a hundred years ago is now fast paced and unpredictable—what Professor Peter Vaill aptly called "permanent whitewater."[7] The world is smaller, and organizations must respond online to developments in a truly global economy. Technological innovation continues to accelerate, as does the rate of development of new products.

Meanwhile, our economy has also become overwhelmingly based on services rather than manufacturing. Manufacturing now accounts for less than 10 percent of jobs in the United States, while service industries account for approximately 80 percent.[8] Even IBM, once dominant in the manufacture of computers, is now primarily in the business of providing business solutions. Service organizations face relatively high levels of uncertainty because their clients' needs and circumstances differ, so these organizations and their employees require considerable flexibility to customize their services to customer requirements.

The upshot is that the number and complexity of the uncertainties facing organizations have overwhelmed the capacity of bureaucratic management. The hierarchy can no longer absorb most of these uncertainties or buffer workers from them, so the wall between workers and the organization's environment has come crashing down. Organizations need workers to take active responsibility for handling more and more of the uncertainties involved in the accomplishment of their purposes. So organizations have been forced to flatten their hierarchies and push decision making down to workers. Workers are called on to adapt to customers' needs, simplify and improve organizational processes, coordinate with other workers and teams, and initiate ideas for new products and services. In short, organizations now depend on workers to use their own judgment and to make many of the decisions formerly made by managers alone.

As decision making has become less centralized, rules and procedures have been dramatically reduced. After all, much of their rationale was to reduce and control worker choice, and organizations now need to give workers the space to make intelligent choices. Consider the old refrain that countless customers heard when encountering bureaucratic requirements that made no sense in their case: "Sorry, I'm just following the rules." That line is no longer acceptable in today's business climate and is being replaced by "Let's see what I can do to help." Flight attendants are generally free now to hand out drinks or snacks during long on-ground delays, for example, instead of sticking to a strict schedule. Likewise, hotel receptionists are increasingly given the leeway to reduce charges to make up for service deficiencies reported by customers. In this new environment, then, it is widely recognized that employee empowerment requires a pushing down of choice and authority to workers to allow them to make intelligent decisions.

The point that I want to emphasize here is that all these changes also require that a strong sense of purpose gets put back into workers' jobs. Workers simply cannot make intelligent choices without having clear task purposes. Workers must also be committed to those purposes. For, as mentioned earlier, the greater judgment of the new work requires a deeper personal commitment than did the old compliance work. For these and other reasons, career counselor Richard Leider has suggested calling the new era the "age of purpose."[9]

The Human Need for Purpose

Fortunately, organizations' needs for committed, purposeful work fit an intense human need for purpose. It is the purpose aspect of the new work that most engages our commitment and stirs our passions. Our workdays may be structured by our work activities, but those activities are given meaning and significance by the purposes they serve. Much of the color in our lives comes from the drama, challenge, struggle—and it is to be hoped the triumph—of handling the uncertainties involved in accomplishing those purposes.

There is a great deal of evidence that people are hardwired to care about purposes. We seem to need to see ourselves as going somewhere—as being on a journey in pursuit of a significant purpose. In *The Hero with a Thousand Faces*, the late Joseph Campbell reported that virtually all cultures have parallel myths about heroic journeys.[10] These journeys involve dramatic difficulties, dangers, periods of despair, and eventual success—always in the service of a worthy purpose. These myths, then, seem to capture an essential part of the human experience.

There is also much evidence that people suffer when they lack purpose. Clinical studies show that people deteriorate in various ways if they are without purpose. This insight first showed up in the survival of concentration camp internees[11] but also seems to be a factor in the survival and well-being of military prisoners of war, people in nursing homes, and even retirees. In the 1960s, the French existentialist movement also drew attention to the psychological emptiness that comes from a lack of purpose. Philosophers like Sartre and Camus pointed out that, without purpose, life becomes meaningless and people experience a sense of alienation and angst. Camus captured this sense of meaninglessness vividly in *The Myth of Sisyphus*.[12] Sisyphus was a king in Greek mythology who had so offended the gods that he was condemned to roll a large stone up a steep hill in Hades only to watch it roll down again and endlessly repeat this cycle. This Greek version of hell was essentially a demanding but meaningless activity with no purpose.

The lack of purpose in the compliance era, then, had significant psychological costs for workers. But generations of workers came to accept this as the nature of work. In his book *Working*, Studs Terkel used the memorable phrase "a Monday through Friday sort of dying" to refer to these costs at their worst.[13] Compliance-era work was a bit like Sisyphus's toil, except that you could go home in the evening and take the weekend off. Workers came to think of this sort of work as a kind of necessary evil (or devil's bargain)—forty to sixty hours a week of meaningless labor in exchange for economic survival. Work was considered an economic cost that left you depleted. It was something to survive rather than enjoy—something to withdraw from emotionally, to numb out from and get through.

In contrast, today's workers—and especially knowledge workers—tend to expect their work to be at least somewhat meaningful and rewarding. They are more educated than workers of the preceding era, have a higher standard of living, and see more opportunities for meaning in the new work.[14] Researchers on generational differences note that younger workers (Generation Xers and millenials) are especially likely to demand meaningful work—and to leave if they do not find the work meaningful. These younger workers also want more freedom to work in their own style, finding their own ways of accomplishing a task purpose.[15]

So today's workforce and the new work combine to produce a growing demand for meaningful work. This demand is becoming a powerful force in the new job market. A number of recent books are aimed at workers who want to change jobs to find work that better serves the purposes they care about. Organizations now find themselves competing to attract and retain workers on the basis of the meaningfulness of their work. I live close enough to Silicon Valley to hear the radio ads stressing the opportunity to move to an organization that offers "exciting projects" that "make a difference."

Purpose-Centered Leadership

As the work environment and worker expectations have changed, our understanding of leadership has gone through a dramatic paradigm shift. Compliance-era models of leadership were based largely on studies of first-line supervisors at a time when managers buffered workers from environmental uncertainties. Likewise, the motivational assumptions behind those models involved exchanges or transactions of extrinsic rewards for performing those activities. These models are now called "transactional" leadership.[16]

By the late 1970s and early 1980s, however, it was clear that these models were no longer adequate. They didn't work for higher-level leadership, and they didn't work when workers had to adapt and change in response to environmental uncertainties. What was missing, of course, was any mention of an overriding and meaningful task purpose.

In the late 1970s, the political scientist James McGregor Burns published an influential study of U.S. presidents who had inspired national change.[17] He found that these presidents had held out a worthy purpose around which the nation could rally. These presidents were also able to articulate a compelling vision of what the future would be like if that purpose were met. The purpose and vision, then, provided a target that could align the efforts of different people to solve problems and cooperate. At the same time, the compelling vision was a strong motivational force that inspired people. Burns emphasized that these meaningful purposes appealed to people's higher nature, rather than to their "lower" needs for self-interest and extrinsic rewards. He called this form of leadership "transformational."

Burns's purpose-centered approach to leadership was soon adapted by management researchers and practitioners. Since the 1980s, a wealth of books on transformational, inspirational, or visionary leadership have been published.[18] The new purpose-centered models of leadership now apply not only to top managers but to team leaders at all organizational levels. Purpose-centered leadership gives workers the information they need to make intelligent decisions and also provides an intrinsically rewarding sense of meaningfulness for their work. Even the rather hierarchical U.S. military has shifted leadership practices to emphasize purpose-centered leadership. Written orders now begin with a "commander's intent" that spells out the purpose behind an order. Knowing the purpose makes the activities more meaningful and also allows individuals to improvise in order to better accomplish the purpose when they encounter unexpected circumstances. (Purpose-centered leadership will be discussed in more detail in part 4 of this book.)

Not All Purposes Are Equally Engaging

Organizational statements of vision followed from purpose-centered leadership and are now very common. Again, they serve both to guide decision making and to gain commitment to a common purpose. Because they are aimed at gaining commitment rather than compliance, these vision statements can't be enacted by fiat and simply pushed down through the organization. You can't delegate commitment, after all—you have to find a purpose that inspires it.

As Burns had learned with U.S. presidents, corporate executives found that not all purposes are equal. Some evoke deeper passions than others. In particular, workers are seldom inspired by economic purposes involving profit—unless the company's welfare is threatened. Rather, inspiration generally comes from deeper values and higher purposes. A good vision statement forces management to dig into the fundamental values that underlie the organization's culture—to understand what the organization stands for.[19] Common themes here are service to customers, a commitment to quality, and a drive for innovation—worthy purposes that people in the organization can take pride in. The organization's vision, then, is a statement of an exciting future that would be meaningful and worthy as judged by those values.

In this way, purpose-centered leadership and workers' needs for meaning have become a force for redefining organizational goals. Although profits and market share remain important, the trend is no longer to see them as paramount. Studies of organizations that have been highly successful over a long period found that these organizations have core ideologies that emphasize "more than profits."[20] One of those researchers used the following analogy to describe the status of economic goals: "[Organizations] need profits in the same way as any living being needs oxygen. It is a necessity to stay alive, but it is not the purpose of life."[21] Peter Block argued that purposes such as customer service and quality are not only more meaningful for workers but are also what put organizations closer to the marketplace to begin with and are therefore what take care of financial issues.[22] Recently, the term "balanced scorecard" has become popular to discuss this broadening of organizational goals to include service to customers and other stakeholders.[23]

For an example of a purpose-driven management philosophy that emphasizes service to multiple stakeholders, see "Purpose-Driven Management: The New West Institute."

Shared Purposes Transform Relationships

One of the benefits of a shared, compelling purpose is that it acts as a "superordinate goal" that promotes collaborative relationships among organizational members—so that people approach issues with the goal of finding a solution that best serves the common

PURPOSE-DRIVEN MANAGEMENT:
THE NEW WEST INSTITUTE

The New West Institute emphasizes purpose-driven management in its consulting and has used the material in this book as a foundation for its work with organizations. Its leaders refer to their management philosophy as The 3rd Way.[24] New West contrasts the 3rd Way with two earlier approaches to management that were driven respectively by (1) deference to heroic bosses who were hoped to have the answers and (2) heavy reliance on programs and policies. In 3rd Way organizations, hierarchies, programs, and policies are seen as being of secondary importance to the organization's purpose in guiding decisions. The shared criterion for a decision, then, is not "what does the boss think?" or "what does the policy say?" but "what would advance the purpose?" Bosses are open to new information when they are wrong, and policies can be revised when they don't advance the purpose.

In spelling out purpose, New West advocates serving the needs of three primary stakeholder groups—clients, owners, and coworkers. Managers and workers seek to find "triple wins" that advance the needs of all three groups—meeting clients' needs, providing profits for owners, and helping to develop coworkers. New West emphasizes that this balancing act requires daily, disciplined attention. The objective is to form long-term relationships with members of each group in order to avoid the costs and volatility of turnover in clients, employees, or stockholders. For each group, then, this objective is pursued through four core processes: *attracting* ideal clients, employees, or stockholders by making promises to them; *fulfilling* these promises by meeting their needs with every contact within the organization; *retaining* them by prizing the future value of the relationships; and *improving* their quality of life by continuing to find ways of benefiting them. Managers and workers jointly commit to "serving the three with the four," that is, serving the three stakeholder groups through the four core business processes. While a business must perform more than these four processes in order to succeed, New West contends that these four core processes provide the essential foundation for that success.

This shared commitment creates a "community of purpose" within the organization. New West finds that managers act less like parents and workers act less like children than under other management philosophies. People treat each other like adults engaged in a common purpose. As New West puts it, "No kids are allowed in the twenty-first century."

purpose. Within a work group, then, a compelling shared purpose transforms the relationships between team members—including the relationship between you, as the leader, and the rest of the team.

In the compliance era, leaders were often forced to act like parents—knowing what was best, making the decisions, and enforcing the rules. The status difference between bosses and subordinates was substantial, decision making was often autocratic, and deference toward bosses and their opinions was expected. In today's work, on the other hand, shared purposes and the need for worker judgment allow workers to be treated more like adults and relationships between you and your team members to be more collaborative and egalitarian. When a common purpose becomes paramount, then, you will want to seek out helpful information from team members, and they will want to help you avoid mistakes.

▪ ▪ ▪

In summary, it's clear that purposes are powerful parts of the new work. The next chapter looks at what is involved in achieving those purposes—the process of self-management.

3

Self-Management in the Pursuit of Purpose

This chapter will give you a detailed understanding of the essence of today's work—self-management. As we'll see, it is the defining characteristic of employee engagement as well as the source of the intrinsic rewards that drive employee engagement.

You'll probably miss the core of today's more purposeful work if you only look at the visible activities or behaviors of this work. You will see only tremendous variety—bookkeeping, counseling, sales, and so on. The common core requirements of the new work aren't behavioral at all—at least not in the traditional way we think of overt, behavioral actions. They involve the mental events that direct those actions toward a purpose.

Consider the way managers talk about the new work. It involves "working smart," "using judgment," "taking responsibility," and "applying your intelligence" toward the organization's purposes. Again, these are mental events. Academics use fancier words to describe this purposive mental activity: *self-regulating, self-controlling,* and *self-managing.* I prefer the term *self-managing* because it conveys the idea that workers now do much of what managers used to do for them. Whatever term you prefer, we are talking about the way that workers add value in the new work.

What's Involved in Self-Management?

Figure 2 shows a flow chart that Erik Jansen and I developed to show the essential events in self-management.[1] The circle represents visible *task activities*—overt task behaviors like planting flowers, grinding lenses, or taking orders over the telephone. The four boxes are the *self-management events* that direct that behavior toward a purpose. Like most flow charts, the diagram oversimplifies what is often an intuitive and messy process. However, it is useful in fleshing out the key parts of self-management.

Figure 2. **Self-Management Diagram**

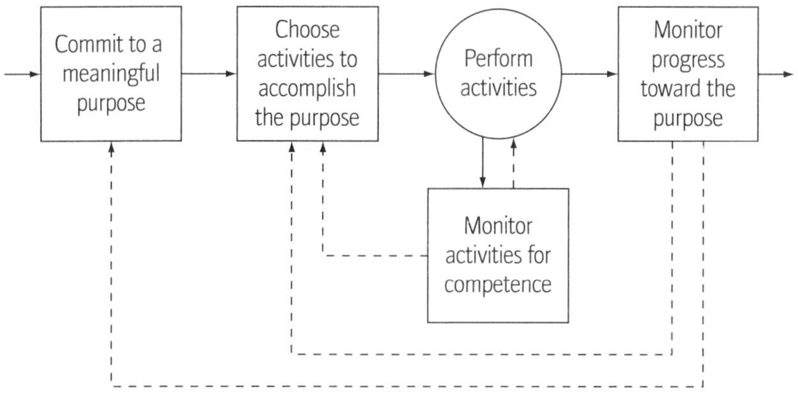

Note: Circle represents overt task behavior. Boxes represent internal (cognitive) self-management events that direct overt behavior. Dotted lines represent feedback effects.

Source: Adapted from Kenneth W. Thomas, Erik Jansen, and Walter G. Tymon Jr., "Navigating in the Realm of Theory: An Empowering View of Construct Development," *Research in Organizational Change and Development* 10 (1997): 1–30. Reprinted by permission of the publisher.

The solid arrows in the figure show the main sequence of events, from left to right. Self-management begins when you commit to a meaningful purpose. You then choose activities to accomplish the purpose. As you perform those activities, you monitor the competence of that performance to make sure that it is adequate. Finally, you monitor progress toward accomplishing the task purpose to make sure that the activities are having the intended effect and are actually moving the purpose forward.

For example, consider a self-managing gardener who works for a landscaping firm. The gardener commits to planting a flower garden that will delight a customer. She chooses which flowers to plant and where to plant them. As she plants them, she monitors her behavior to make sure the plants have proper soil, that their root balls are properly covered, and that they receive enough water. Periodically, she checks with the customer to make sure that the customer is actually delighted with how the garden is taking shape.

The dotted lines in the figure are feedback effects. They represent adjustments and learnings during the course of a task. For example, if activities aren't being performed well enough, you can adjust your performance or, if that doesn't work, you can choose other activities. Likewise, if the purpose isn't being accomplished, you can look for new activities that will move the task forward.

The next sections go into more detail about each of the events in self-management, to help you understand better what today's work requires.

Committing to a Meaningful Purpose

Without commitment to a purpose, there would be no point in the remaining events. There would be no reason to make choices, care about the competence of one's work behavior, or keep track of progress. In many ways, then, this commitment drives the entire self-management process.

So what is commitment? Commitment to a purpose is inspired by the pull of a worthy, desirable purpose. But commitment is clearly more than desiring or hoping that the purpose will be achieved. It is a decision to take personal responsibility for making it happen. Let me spell out this distinction because it is important. Much decision making is activity centered rather than purpose centered. In activity-centered decision making, we decide to perform behaviors with the hope that they will accomplish a purpose. The purpose is in the background as a desire, intention, or aim. We perform the activities and see what happens. If those activities don't achieve the purpose, we are disappointed, but that is sometimes the nature of life, and we move on to another task.

In purpose-centered decision making, by contrast, we commit to a purpose, and the activities are in the background. That is, we're not entirely sure how we will accomplish the purpose. The decision is basically to find the activities needed to deal with the uncertainties involved. Subject to our moral code and our other commitments, we are deciding to do whatever is needed to accomplish the purpose.

The nature of commitment became clearest to me when I approached marriage, so I'll use that as an analogy. I could have made a reasonable effort to make the relationship succeed and then waited to see how well that worked. But I realized that this wait-and-see approach would have real consequences: it would make it less likely that the relationship would succeed and would also make it less likely that my wife-to-be would commit to making it work. I realized that I already knew enough about my future wife to make a commitment and that I needed to do so. So I made the commitment—to myself and to her. And we both began to use the language of commitment: "We will work it out."

We committed to doing whatever it took to make the marriage successful—to keep track of how well it was working and to find ways of overcoming obstacles.

As the marriage analogy implies, committing to any purpose is not to be taken lightly. It is a promise you make to yourself and to others that involves some personal accountability: you will be unhappy with yourself if you fail to deliver. People grieve when forced to abandon a commitment—it's like suffering a small death. Taking on a new commitment also involves investing a significant chunk of psychological energy in a task purpose. It is possible to become overcommitted—to feel too thinly stretched to function. At those times, you need to complete some of your tasks or get them back on track before you can find the energy to take on new ones.

Nevertheless, commitment is what we all need if we are to be effective in accomplishing the purposes we care about in an era of increasing uncertainties. General Gordon Sullivan, former Army Chief of Staff, put it well in the title of his book with Michael Harper: *Hope Is Not a Method*.[2]

Choosing Activities to Accomplish the Purpose

After committing to a purpose, the second event in self-management is deciding how to make the purpose happen—selecting activities that will accomplish it. Notice that commitment depends on this ability to choose and vice versa. Without the freedom to choose proper activities, it would be pointless to commit to a purpose—to take personal responsibility for achieving it. You could not steer your behavior toward the purpose. You could only carry out prescribed activities as well as possible and hope that they would achieve the purpose. Likewise, without a committed purpose to steer it, choice becomes choice for its own sake and degrades into simple whim or impulse.

Allowing workers to choose useful activities is the main point of the decentralized decision making in the new work. Workers use their intelligence in problem solving to find ways of dealing with the uncertainties they encounter: what would be a good way of achieving the task purpose given the circumstances they find? In self-management, workers tailor their work activities to the needs of the situation in ways that fixed rules cannot anticipate. Workers select appropriate work procedures and adapt or improve old procedures—or invent new ones—depending on the changing requirements of the task.

Choice involves freedom of thought—being able to act out of one's own understanding of the situation. The elaborate rules of the compliance era were intended to box in workers' judgment and behavior. I once saw a safety poster that actually said "Don't Think!"—implying that free thought was dangerous. In contrast, managers in the new-work world are encouraging workers to think "outside the box." This "box" is made up of the old constraints on thinking: the elaborate rules, the established procedures and precedents, and the tradition of relying on the boss's judgment rather than their own and of using prevailing assumptions instead of their own understanding. The freedom of thought of committed workers has become a vital competitive resource that produces inventions, innovations, continuous improvement, renewal, and customer satisfaction.

Monitoring for Competence

After choosing our activities, we begin to perform them. As we do so, the next event in self-management comes into play—monitoring our performance for competence. This event, then, involves making sure that our work activities meet our standards.

During the compliance era, work standards were external and set by managers at fixed levels. Workers were charged with doing work that met these levels—doing "good enough" or "satisfactory" work. In contrast, self-management involves committed workers' meeting their own internal standards of competence. Internal standards are more dynamic: people raise their standards on tasks they care about as they become more skilled and experienced at the task activities. Worker self-monitoring, then, can be a powerful force for improving performance.

The nature of the standards involved in self-monitoring depends on the type of activity involved. For a machinist, standards involve criteria such as the measurement specifications of a part, its finish, and the absence of any burrs. For a salesperson making a presentation to a group, the standards would be quite different: keeping the group's interest, conveying essential information, listening, answering questions, and remaining courteous. Standards generally cover aspects of activities that play a significant role in achieving the task purpose. Most of these standards are technical standards—standards relating to technique—but ethical standards may also be involved. The notion of worker *professionalism* includes both.

Regardless of the nature of the standards, the essential requirements of monitoring for competence are the same. People must pay attention to how well their standards are being met by being fully present, involved, and focused and by concentrating on the task. They must also be prepared to make adjustments in their performance of the activity when threats and opportunities (uncertainties) arise. The machinist changes a machine setting and spends more time polishing a part as necessary; the salesperson rephrases a statement and provides a different example in response to a customer question. Some of these adjustments may involve stopping to think, but with experience much of the adjustment becomes intuitive. As workers become more adept at the task, the activities and adjustments often blend more smoothly into a seamless and graceful flow.

Monitoring for Progress

The last event in the self-management process involves checking to see that the activities are actually accomplishing the purpose—that progress is being made. Like monitoring for competence of performance, this step involves an assessment of how the task is going, together with a willingness to take action to make changes. In contrast to monitoring competence, however, monitoring progress is a purpose-centered evaluation of how well the task is going.

I find that people sometimes miss this distinction, so I'll elaborate a bit. There are two parts to evaluating how the task is going—how well you are performing the activities (competence of performance) and how well the activities are accomplishing the task purpose (progress toward the purpose). Both are important. If you have chosen the right activities, the competence of your performance is likely to advance the purpose. In an uncertain world, however, you can't be sure that those activities are the right ones. So you have to keep checking to make sure that the purpose is being achieved. This is, after all, the bottom line of the task. Without monitoring for progress, you are only hoping that the task is on track.

Since most purposes involve helping an internal or external customer, monitoring task progress usually involves some form of customer feedback. On longer tasks, this means checking with the customer at different milestones and making any needed adjustments. The gardener, for example, checks with the customer at key points in the planning and planting of a garden. On shorter, more repetitive tasks, monitoring means checking with customers after they receive a product or service and using that information to improve task activities to increase customer satisfaction in the future. The machinist learns whether the finished part works for a customer, and the salesperson finds out whether the customer makes a purchase. This use of customer feedback became a cornerstone of much of the quality movement.

Measuring progress and collecting feedback from customers takes a certain amount of discipline. It takes time and energy away from performing task activities. There is also some psychological cost to reexamining your choices, exposing them to customer evaluation, and possibly having to make changes in your activities. But it's the only way for a committed worker to be sure the purpose is being achieved. Again, it's dramatic to contrast this aspect of self-management with the conventional wisdom of the compliance era, which concluded that "workers resist change." Looking back, the truth was more that, under command-and-control management, workers often resisted imposed change. In the new work, committed workers initiate changes when their purpose is threatened or they see a better way of accomplishing it.[3]

Feedback and Learning

Finally, consider the rather innocent-looking feedback arrows in figure 2. In reality, these arrows represent much of the value-added of human intelligence in dealing with task uncertainties.

Feedback comes from the two monitoring events—monitoring for competence of performance and for progress toward the purpose. Think of this feedback as either positive or negative. When feedback is positive, it means that our efforts are working as we expected, resulting in competently performed activities, and those activities are moving the purpose forward. Positive feedback strengthens our work habits and our assumptions about what works, as well as our commitment to the purpose. That's good, of course, but we could program machines to do all of our work if these habits and assumptions always worked.

The real value of human intelligence shows up when the feedback is negative—when something isn't working. After all, that's how uncertainties show up in tasks: the expected doesn't happen. According to American educator John Dewey, that was also when learning was most likely to occur.[4] When our processes don't work, we look up to see what happened, try to figure out why, and come to a new understanding that is usually more complex than what we believed before. The new understanding leads to a new activity or adjustment. If that works, our new understanding is strengthened—until we encounter a new uncertainty, and the learning cycle repeats itself. If something doesn't work, we keep trying to figure it out until we find something that works. If nothing works after a great deal of effort and experimentation, our commitment eventually declines, and—sadder but wiser—we move on to a new purpose.

Not only does this feedback produce more responsive and adaptive behavior, then, it also produces important forms of learning. As the work world has become more uncertain, organizations have realized the competitive value of this learning as a kind of intellectual capital and have recognized the importance of becoming a "learning organization," to use Peter Senge's phrase.[5] It has become clearer that workers' learnings in the new work increase their value as human resources and make them more difficult to replace. It has also become clear that organizations need to invest resources in trying to capture or "harvest" this learning and in sharing it with others in the organization who would find it helpful. Some of the learning is in the form of preconscious intuition and the physical artistry of a craftsman. But other learnings are more easily transferable. Some take the form of "lessons learned"—insights or theories that can be told to others. Others are specific innovations or inventions that can be used by others—new techniques or procedures or new physical equipment.

Work Engagement

With that background in the nature of the new work, we are now ready to define "worker engagement." Simply put, *workers are engaged in the new work to the extent that they are actively self-managing at that work.* Rather than simply going through the motions or doing "good enough" work, then, workers are engaged in their work when they are committed to a purpose, using their intelligence to make choices about how to best accomplish the task, monitoring their behavior to make sure they are doing the task well, checking to make sure their actions are actually accomplishing the purpose, and taking corrective action when needed. As mentioned before, this is the way that workers add value in the new work. To borrow a phrase used by the Conference Board and the New West Institute, it is also the way that workers exercise "discretionary control over their performance."[6]

What Happens to Managerial Control?

Notice that the self-management events in figure 2 substitute for some of the traditional command-and-control activities performed by managers—deciding on a task purpose, assigning task activities to workers, supervising or directing those work activities to ensure they are done properly, and making sure that the purpose gets achieved. Many leaders who were used to command-and-control, then, have felt like they were losing control when their organization shifted to worker self-management. In reality, the shift represents a *change* of form for managerial control, rather than a *loss* of it. More of the nuts-and-bolts decision making is taken on by workers, but you, as a leader, stay informed on issues of performance competence and progress.

Under worker self-management, you keep influencing workers, although the form of that influence also shifts. You tend to use less authority and coercion to impose decisions and provide more information and expert advice as inputs to workers' decision making. Several writers have used the metaphor of *partnership* to describe this relationship, underscoring the free flow of information between leader and team member as partners in the task purpose. A number of management writers have also used the metaphor of *coaching* to describe this new relationship.[7] As workers take responsibility for task purposes, they are more likely to welcome this helpful input and to seek it out—in the way that athletes welcome help from a knowledgeable coach. Jack Welch used the metaphor of *boundarylessness* at G.E. to describe this flow of helpful information and the removal of traditional barriers that interfere with it.[8]

It may be helpful for you to remember that the switch to worker self-management is occurring because it is a way to *increase control* over the uncertainties facing a work team. By allowing workers to make more decisions on task uncertainties they encounter, you are better able to leverage your time to deal with larger uncertainties facing the team. You can attend to planning, watch for dangers and opportunities facing the team, help with coordination, deal with personnel issues, and make sure that nothing important falls through the cracks.

As a practical manner, it's also important to remember that you retain your command-and-control authority and can use it if needed. As Peter Block noted, self-managing workers have the right to disagree with their leader's suggestions, but the leader also retains "51 percent" of the votes in the final decision when there is disagreement on an important issue.[9] The challenge for you, of course, is to lead in such a way that this overruling occurs fairly rarely—or else self-management becomes a sham.

All this assumes that your workers are ready for self-management. That brings us to the subject of worker development.

Worker Development

In a paper with Susan Hocevar and Gail Thomas, I proposed that *development* simply means moving toward greater self-management.[10] Think about this for a moment. Isn't that what we look for as our children develop and what we mean by maturity? We look for young people to increasingly commit to worthwhile purposes and accept responsibility for them, to make their own decisions consistent with those purposes, to apply standards to their behavior, and to be resourceful and persistent in pursuing their purposes. Those are the kinds of lessons we try to teach our children and the way we judge how responsible a young person is becoming. As parents, this is also what guides us in deciding how much self-management to allow our children as they grow up.

In many ways, then, self-management is simply a way of describing the task capabilities of an adult human being. To be self-managing at work is to fully engage those adult capabilities in one's work tasks.

Still, workers don't always come to a task ready to be fully self-managing. Younger workers may still be learning general self-management skills. Some workers of any age may be hesitant to self-manage, particularly if they are emerging from an environment with command-and-control management. Even workers who are predisposed to be self-managing may need to ease into it on new tasks as they learn new skills and gain experience.

Other workers start to self-manage, run into difficulties, and become discouraged.

The development of worker self-management, then, is an important issue for leaders in today's work world. It is also an important issue for workers themselves—the key to their effectiveness and satisfaction, their level of responsibility, and even their long-term employability.

This brings us to the central motivational issues of this book. What are the intrinsic rewards that you can use to reinforce self-management and develop self-management skills? How can you and your workers increase those rewards so that engagement and self-management flourish?

PART TWO

The Intrinsic Rewards That Drive Engagement

$\mathcal{A}$ Management Tale, continued

THE WISE CONSULTANT traveled widely to talk with the new workers and returned to share his learnings. He told the executives of the more Purposeful nature of the new work and of the active Self-Management required for worker Engagement, and the executives could see that this was so.

"What, then, is the key to this Engagement?" asked the executives. "Is it Money for their value-added?"

"You need to provide Fair Pay, of course, and Training for skills. For there are other employers who will provide these if you do not. But I have learned that the key to Engagement is not money. It has more to do with the Heart."

The executives bade him explain, so the consultant continued. "In truth, to actively self-manage is Demanding for them. But they are not opposed to such demands. After all, most are parents and give much of themselves in that way. What they crave—in work as in parenting—is the sense that they make a Positive Difference in something of value. They long to feel that their Conscientiousness is making a Contribution on life's stage—that their efforts are advancing a Worthy Purpose. They are Fulfilled, and their Engagement Sustained when their Self-Management is effective in such a cause. Then their work truly gives back to them. But, alas, they become Bitter and Dispirited when their Conscientiousness seems for naught."

Again, the executives heard in this message the echoes of their own motivation. "This has the ring of truth for us," they said. "Yet it is very general. To manage for Engagement, we will need to know more. What exactly do workers need from their work, that we may better enable it?"

"Ah," said the consultant, "this is the key. The rewards that power workers' engagement come from the very steps of their Self-Management. For in Self-Management, they make ongoing judgments of the Meaningfulness of their purpose, the Choice allowed them, the Competence of their activities, and the Progress being made. These four judgments, when they are positive, *are* the Rewards that drive Engagement. These are the things you must attend to, for their effects are most Powerful."

4

Four Intrinsic Rewards

MEANINGFULNESS, CHOICE, COMPETENCE, AND PROGRESS

This part of the book will introduce you to the four intrinsic rewards that drive employee engagement, give you an understanding of their powerful effects, and provide you with a diagnostic framework you can use to build those rewards.

The Four Intrinsic Rewards

During the compliance era when work was less meaningful, managers were forced to think about how they could make workers care about their work. So their motivational arsenal depended heavily on using rewards and punishments that were extrinsic to the work itself and on applying direct social pressure. It would likely surprise those old-school managers to learn that the key rewards that drive worker engagement today come directly from engagement itself—from the steps involved in active self-management that we discussed in the last chapter.

How is that possible?

Each of the events in the self-management process requires the worker to make a judgment—of the meaningfulness of the task purpose, the degree of choice available in selecting activities, how competently he or she is performing those activities, and the amount of progress being made toward the task purpose.[1] These four judgments, then, are logical requirements of self-management. But they are much more than that. They are not detached, arm's-length judgments—they carry a strong emotional charge. When the judgments are positive, their emotional charges *are* the intrinsic rewards of self-management—the emotional "juices" that energize and reinforce continued engagement.[2] In our research, Walt Tymon and I have found it helpful to refer to these emotional charges, or feelings, as a "*sense* of meaningfulness," "a *sense* of choice," and so on.[3]

So people feel good or excited about a task—whether it produces a quiet glow of satisfaction or an exuberant celebration—when these judgments are positive. Try that idea on for a while. When you feel particularly good about your work, doesn't it have something to do with realizing you're doing something worthwhile (meaningfulness), being able to do something the way you think it should be done (choice), performing some activity particularly well (competence), or making a significant advance toward accomplishing your purpose (progress)?

Figure 3 shows two ways of grouping these four intrinsic rewards.

First, as shown in the rows of the figure, two of the rewards involve *purpose* and two involve *activities*. The sense of meaningfulness and the sense of progress have to do with purpose—the degree to which the work purpose is important or worthy and the degree to which it is actually being accomplished, respectively. In contrast, the sense of choice and the sense of competence come from work activities—from being able to choose the activities that make sense and from performing those activities well.

Figure 3. **The Four Intrinsic Rewards**

	Opportunity rewards	**Accomplishment** rewards
From task **activities**	Sense of **choice**	Sense of **competence**
From task **purpose**	Sense of **meaningfulness**	Sense of **progress**

Source: Modified and reproduced by special permission of the publisher, CPP, Mountain View, CA from *Work Engagement Profile* by Kenneth W. Thomas and Walter G. Tymon, Jr. Copyright 2009 by CPP, Inc. All rights reserved. Duplication in whole or part prohibited.

Second, the columns in the figure show that two of the rewards involve *opportunities* and two involve *accomplishments*. The senses of choice and of meaningfulness are feelings of work opportunity—being able to use your judgment and to pursue a worthwhile purpose, respectively—and come from the early steps of the self-management process. They convey the idea that this is good work to be doing—that performing these activities and pursuing this purpose are worth doing. The senses of competence and of progress, on the other hand, are feelings of accomplishment related to the performance of activities and attainment of the purpose, respectively. These two rewards come from the monitoring steps that occur later in the self-management process and provide the idea that the work is going well. Together, then, the four intrinsic rewards capture the feeling that you are actually accomplishing work that is significant and worthwhile. (For information on how these four rewards build on earlier models of intrinsic motivation, see resource A at the end of the book.)

Here are brief descriptions of the four intrinsic rewards, in the order they occur during the self-management process. They are adapted from the *Work Engagement Profile* (*WEP*) that Walt Tymon and I developed to measure them.[4]

- A sense of *meaningfulness* is the opportunity you feel to pursue a worthy purpose. The feeling of meaningfulness is the feeling that you are on a path that is worth your time and energy—that you are on a valuable mission and that your purpose matters in the larger scheme of things.
- A sense of *choice* is the opportunity you feel to select activities that make sense to you and to perform them in ways that seem appropriate. The feeling of choice is the feeling of being able to use your own judgment and act out of your own understanding.
- A sense of *competence* is the accomplishment you feel in skill-fully performing the activities you have chosen. The feeling of competence involves the sense that you are doing good, high-quality work.
- A sense of *progress* is the accomplishment you feel in achieving the purpose. The feeling of progress involves the sense that your work is moving forward, that your activities are really accomplishing something.

Let's look at why these intrinsic rewards are important to people, and why they carry such strong positive feelings.

Sense of Meaningfulness

I used to say that meaningful purposes were the ones that fit people's values. But meaningfulness is about the energy attached to a purpose, and *values* seems too dry of a word to capture that. The word *passion* conveys that sense of energy better, as in "a passion for ____." Meaningfulness, then, is about the passion you have for a task purpose.

People's passions tend to develop and change a bit over their work lives.[5] Younger workers are deeply involved in learning the ropes about their work (and about life in general). So at that stage of life, their passions at work often involve showing that they can handle things. The phrases that describe these passions convey the sense that they are being tested and have something to prove: being able to "cut the mustard," "find their sea legs," "stand on their own two feet," "make a go of it," "earn their keep," or "make the grade."

But as workers begin to complete this stage and to realize that they *can* do the work, their passions tend to shift. They commonly have a "crisis of meaning" at this point, and they begin to need more from their work and lives. The work often feels empty, and workers find that they need to answer a new set of questions: "Okay, I can do the work. Now what do I want to do? Why?" In struggling with these questions, workers begin to discover their particular areas of passion for work and to find those purposes that have meaning for them and that sustain them emotionally.

There is a fair amount of diversity in people's passions, in part because they are influenced by personal history. For example, both of my otherwise loving parents were not very good at listening. I find now that I have a passion for communicating ideas, which fires me up in the classroom and is sustaining me through the writing of this book. My friends, who have different histories, find great meaning in other types of purposes: fighting injustice, making beautiful things, pushing technological advances, getting teams to pull together, or making useful things with their hands. In any organization, this diversity of passion means that it is important to match individuals with the tasks that have meaning for them. This involves getting to know people's passions, making judicious task assignments, and asking for volunteers when possible—to allow workers to do their own matching of passions to tasks.[6]

However, there is also a considerable amount of commonality of passion within most work groups—not totally, but enough to make it possible for groups to be energized by a shared, meaningful purpose. Some of this commonality comes from workers' self-selecting into fields of work that match their passions, and some comes from shared work history in the group. For example, some work groups will have a shared passion to develop a new product they believe in, or to develop a report that "knocks people's socks off."

Finally, shared passions also cut across individuals and organizations. The deepest of these are *spiritual* passions. I am not talking about spiritual in the sense of organized religion here, although religions speak directly to these passions. Rather, I am talking about a deeply felt desire to have one's life make a difference in the larger scheme of things, to make a contribution, to lead a worthy life that one can be proud of, to be "on the right path."[7] As noted earlier, these passions often show up in terms of being of service to customers and of bettering society or people's lives in some way. In my case, then, my passion for communicating ideas has merged with a desire to help people: my deepest satisfaction in work is to give people insights that help their lives work better.

I invite you to stop for a minute to think about your own passions. What gets you excited at work? What touches you deeply?

Sense of Choice

The experience of choice is connected to our early experiences with authority.[8] Children are *dependent* upon parents, older siblings, and other authority figures. On the whole (but with exceptions, as every parent knows), children learn to comply with the requests of those authorities. We learn that these authorities know more about many things and control resources that are important to us, and we come to accept their right to make many decisions for us. In this position of dependency, we learn to be sensitive to authorities' desires, and we feel a pressure to satisfy them and to comply with their directions. Later, as teenagers, we commonly go through periods of *counterdependence* or rebellion. At this point, we discover that our own judgments have value and that parents and other authorities are fallible. So we go through periods of looking for—and reacting against—any behavior by authority figures that appears arbitrary or unfair. Ideally, most of us get through that stage and reach a more adult sense of *interdependence*. In that state, we realize that we and authorities both have useful but imperfect insights, and we work together to accomplish shared goals. We exchange information and views with managers, accept the need for them to make final decisions on some issues, and use our own judgment to carry out tasks over which we have some autonomy. Here, relations with managers have more of the quality of respect between adults rather than parent-child paternalism and dependency.

With this background, it isn't hard to see why the experience of choice is emotionally loaded for us and why a sense of choice is intrinsically rewarding. It's partly about feeling grown up. Chris Argyris began pointing out in the late 1950s that traditional management could stunt workers' development and keep them in a state of dependency.[9] Today, psychologists also show

53

how being treated in paternalistic or controlling ways can make us relive childhood feelings.[10] We are likely to feel like children (small, dependent) or teenagers (resentful, rebellious) when we are told what to do and when our ideas are not listened to. In contrast, we feel more like adults when we exercise choice and are listened to. The notion of being able to make choices is so central to the experience of being an adult that a number of writers define the *self* as the part of us that chooses.[11] Exercising choice is fundamental to the way we attempt to control events in our lives. The psychologist Richard deCharms described the experience of choice as the feeling of being the "origin" of one's own behavior, in contrast to the feeling of being a "pawn" of external events and forces.[12] In a very real way, then, we lose our sense of self when we are not able to make choices—and we shut down emotionally and disengage from the task.

Choice takes on extra importance when we are committed to a meaningful purpose. Then a sense of choice means *being able to do what makes sense to you to accomplish the purpose*. It means being able to use your intelligence, take the best course of action, and make effective use of your time. In short, choice allows you to be performing those activities that you experience as useful. When you are not free to choose, on the other hand, you often find yourself trying to accomplish your work in ways that seem silly or like a waste of time—with resulting frustration. It is impressive how much frustration you can discover in many committed people by asking them about the pointless rules or directives that interfere with their work.

Finally, a sense of choice also gives you a feeling of ownership of the task. When you make choices about how to perform a task, you redesign it to some degree, and it becomes your own. You also feel personally responsible for task accomplishment—for the quality of your activities and the progress you make toward the purpose.[13] After all, if quality and progress result from *your* decisions, you deserve to feel proud of those accomplishments. The opposite is true for having a low sense of choice. I find that few micromanagers seem to understand this. If a boss insists on making detailed decisions for workers and events go badly, it isn't surprising that workers feel less responsible for the outcome than the manager would like. It was the boss's decisions that produced the result, not their own; they had little control over events.

Sense of Competence

Performing task activities is the most visible part of most jobs, so many writers have offered explanations of what makes this performance rewarding. A number of related terms have been used, including competence, mastery, and artistry. I'm using the more established term *competence*, but this intrinsic reward is complex and often includes bits of those other related feelings as well.

The idea that performing activities well is intrinsically rewarding became popular in the late 1950s, when psychologist Robert W. White wrote a classic article, "Motivation Reconsidered: The Concept of Competence."[14] Even infants, he noted, take pleasure in learning to master skills and keep repeating tasks for the *simple pleasure of doing them well.* This sense of competence motivation, he argued, is built into all of us to help us acquire the skills that we need to survive and to thrive as a species. In the 1970s, Edward Deci began publishing psychological research that showed how a sense of competence can keep people engaged in anagrams (word scrambles) and other activities.[15] (Deci's model is briefly described in resource A.) Getting positive feedback about doing something well is often enough to keep people performing an activity—doing it for the sheer pleasure of enjoying the resulting feelings of competence. The power of this reward is apparent in the universal popularity of recreational games. There are even a number of pastimes—like spectator sports and some performing arts—where much of our reward comes from the pleasure we get in seeing *other* people show great competence.

In the context of a meaningful purpose, performing activities well takes on an added significance. If you are pursuing a meaningful purpose, and you have chosen activities that you believe will accomplish that purpose, then performing those activities well also means that you are *serving that purpose*. In other words, you are aware that performing well is making an important difference in achieving something you care about. Consider surgeons at work in an operating room. They may be enjoying their skill and dexterity, but a large part of that enjoyment is in knowing that the competence of their actions is helping a patient.

I find that some of the sense of competence also involves a kind of aesthetic or artistic satisfaction, as though we were all artists working in different media. That is certainly true for me as I am writing this section of the book. I am trying my best to express these ideas clearly—to clarify the ideas and to pick the right words—and to make the sentences flow. When it seems to be going well, I feel a sense of artistry that helps to sustain me. My inner voice says things like "Yes, that's a nice sentence" with an intensity that ranges from satisfaction to excitement. Consultant Dick Richards has described this experience of artistry in his wonderful little book *Artful Work*.[16] Like artists, we gradually master the fundamentals of our various crafts—that is, we learn to be technically sound—and then learn to improvise and create new variations to meet the uncertainties that the new work brings us. We are used to the idea of craft workers' being artisans, so that the word *craftsmanship* suggests a kind of artistry. However, service work can also involve artistry. For example, there is a competent way of handling difficult customers that I can only describe as graceful. The same is true for skilled teachers. The relationship between competence and artistry also holds for managerial jobs, as spelled out in Peter Vaill's book, *Managing as a Performing Art.*[17]

Research also shows that we tend to be most engaged in the task when we are performing activities most competently—having all our attention on meeting the challenge helps us perform well but is also a positive experience in itself. It is characteristic of peak performance.[18] When people become fully engaged in doing good work, they often become so engrossed in the task that they lose track of time and are surprised to learn how quickly it has flown by.

Finally, we may also have feelings of virtue when we are meeting our own standards of competent performance. We stand a little taller as we feel that we are "doing it right."

Sense of Progress

Children tend to have an obvious and touching hunger for immediate gratification. On a car trip, they continually ask, "Are we there yet?" They want to be there now—wherever they are going. As people grow into adults, they generally learn to take on longer tasks and develop patience. But the need for reinforcement doesn't go away; it simply changes form. The childhood need to "be there now" evolves into the need to feel that you are getting there—that you are making progress. Monitoring the progress you are making on the task purpose is the final element of the self-management process discussed in chapter 3. In many ways, progress is the bottom line of purposeful work. Is the purpose being realized or not, and how quickly? Having a meaningful purpose can be enough for you to begin a task with enthusiasm, but you need to keep experiencing a sense of progress toward that purpose in order to sustain that enthusiasm.

Some people ask me whether the ultimate intrinsic reward doesn't come from actually accomplishing the purpose—from the thrill of crossing the finish line. It is true that you may have the most intense positive feelings at that moment. For most meaningful purposes, however, climactic moments like this are a very small portion of your time on a task. Olympic athletes, for example, prepare for years for their brief moment of victory—and most of them lose the race or fail to make the team. It clearly takes some reinforcement along the way to keep them going. In addition, many task purposes don't seem to have clear-cut finish lines. For example, committee members may identify an important problem, collect information, draft a report, brief their recommendations to another group, see actions taken, and observe the gradual effects of those actions. Rather than having one big moment of triumph, they take a series of smaller steps forward—what Tom Peters called "little wins."[19] On a day-to-day basis, then, it is this evidence of progress that keeps people going. So it seems more accurate to talk about a general need to make progress on a task and to treat the final completion of the task as just one step in that progress.

Consider how central the notion of progress (or lack of it) is to our experience of our work and of our lives as a whole. As discussed in chapter 2, people seem hardwired to think of themselves as on journeys. We ask each other, "How's it going?" We answer with phrases like "moving forward," "on track," "moving ahead," or "getting there." If we feel no sense of progress, we say we are "stuck," "at a standstill," "in a rut," "going nowhere," or perhaps even "losing ground" or "backsliding." You can probably think of other words that capture this sense of progress.

The *rate* of progress on a task is also important. Jack Welch, former CEO of General Electric, spoke vividly of the energy that he and his employees got from moving forward quickly on work tasks. "Speed," he said simply, "is exhilarating!"[20] Again, think of the words people use to describe their rate of progress on tasks. If progress is swift, we use terms like "stepping out," "cooking," or "smoking." If slow, we use other phrases: "plodding" or "barely making headway." Feel the difference in energy level between *plodding* and *cooking*.

Feelings of progress are problematic for many types of jobs. For example, I recall a workshop that Walt Tymon and I gave at a meeting of human resource professionals. When they completed our *Work Engagement Profile*,[21] they scored relatively low on a sense of progress. This was an important insight for them and helped them to identify more clearly the vague sense they had that something was missing in their work. In the discussion that followed, they were able to pin down several building blocks for progress that were missing in their work—milestones, measurement of improvements, and celebrations—and to identify action steps they could take to provide them.

Feelings of progress are sometimes problematic for managers as well. In the 1980s, for example, psychologist Harry Levinson wrote a classic article titled "When Executives Burn Out."[22] In it he referred to the "special kind of exhaustion" that managers are likely to feel when they expend energy with few visible results.

▪ ▪ ▪

Now that we've examined these four intrinsic rewards and why they are important, we'll look next at how they work—and their effects.

5

How the Intrinsic Rewards Work—and Their Effects

This chapter will help you reexamine some old half-truths about motivation, give you a basic understanding of how the intrinsic rewards work, and provide you with some research findings on the widespread benefits of those rewards in the workplace.

Let's start with some common, but misleading, assumptions about motivation.

If you are like me, the notion that you are energized or de-energized by your work fits your experience—it rings true at a gut level. When I first heard this idea, however, I remember that it had a flavor of New Age mysticism. (Is it psychic energy? I wondered.) I now realize that the idea seemed strange to me because it did not fit the rational-economic model that had long dominated thinking about work motivation. Management had several generations to perfect the motivation of compliance. Over this time, the rational-economic thinking that underlies compliance motivation became so ingrained that it seemed self-evident.

There is also a pervasive bias in the public at large that supports that tendency. Research shows that people are quick to recognize the importance of intrinsic rewards in their own behavior but tend to assume that others are motivated by economic "deals" and personal gain,[1] so it is worth spending some time here to understand the limitations of rational-economic assumptions about motivation and to understand how intrinsic motivation works—in others as well as oneself.

Rational-Economic Thinking and Its Limitations

Herbert Simon, the Nobel Prize–winning economist, described the rational model of decision making as follows.[2] When people make choices, they first identify their alternatives. They then consider the likely outcomes of each alternative and the desirability ("utility") of those outcomes. Finally, they choose the alternative that would lead to the most desirable outcome. In simpler terms, *the assumption is that people choose behaviors based on their anticipated consequences.* This is pretty familiar stuff: it is the foundation of cost/benefit analysis and pervades management education. Even in the most psychological of management courses, the dominant motivational model has been "expectancy theory," which explains workers' motivation in this way.[3]

For most of us who received this sort of training, the rational model became an automatic way of understanding behavior. And for a long time, it worked: the rational model fit the needs of compliance-era management very well. With workers choosing to attend work, to produce, and to follow the rules largely because of extrinsic outcomes, managers could use the rational model to design reward systems to "incentivize" those behaviors—trying to make sure that desired behaviors would result in economic rewards.

Now, with intrinsic rewards becoming more important, we need to loosen the grip the rational-economic model has on our thinking by recognizing its limitations. Economics is powerful in the consistency of its rational model and in its mathematical tools. However, it is more vulnerable in the fit between its assumptions and actual human behavior. Here, it screens out some motivational realities that are vital to intrinsic motivation.

Consider the following points about intrinsic motivation that go beyond rational-economic thinking.

Point 1: People care about more than money and self-interest at work

As sociologists like Amatai Etzioni have pointed out, people not only strive for financial outcomes, they also try to *do the right thing*, even though it occasionally costs them financially to do so.[4] Theorists like Edgar Schein at MIT and the late Abraham Maslow also pointed out that workers have "higher-order" personal needs that shape behavior.[5] Some of the most significant work rewards come from transpersonal motives, such as helping others. For example, I often do an exercise in which I ask people to recall when they were feeling particularly great about their work. They often pick times when people depended upon them, and they were able to come through. Try this exercise yourself; it's an eye-opener.

If you stick with traditional economic assumptions about work, you're also likely to assume that working is a *cost* for workers. If you buy into that assumption, it leads to a number of other conclusions that make it hard to think intelligently about intrinsic rewards. It suggests, for example, that workers don't want to work, want leisure instead, and will retire as soon as they can afford it. All these conclusions appear to be extremely questionable for the new work and can be dangerously self-fulfilling. It isn't true that work is a cost. *Unrewarding* work is a cost. Rewarding work, on the other hand, is also a good—something one seeks and "consumes." People have a desire to be engaged in meaningful work—to be doing something they experience as worthwhile and fulfilling. While leisure is welcome in moderate doses, especially after long periods of work, it gets old by itself. People need tasks to structure their days and to provide purpose—something of significance to engage them.

Point 2: Intrinsic motivation involves rewards you are getting right now

Another limitation of the rational-economic model comes from the idea of rationality itself. The rational model does not include the experience of getting or enjoying rewards! It's basically a decision-making model. It involves desiring rewarding outcomes in the future, figuring out how to maximize them, and deciding to strive to get them. But it is not concerned with whether or not you are being rewarded now—whether you are enjoying your work. In the rational model, the present moment is a time to calculate and make decisions so that the future can be desirable and to strive to attain that desirable future. Rationality is based on a logic of delayed gratification, which feeds all too well into our culture's puritanism and our Protestant work ethic: "This is serious stuff we're doing here; the future is at stake." This is a pretty barren theoretical landscape for spotting intrinsic rewards!

In technical terms, economics is driven by *prospective rationality*. To understand how the work experience can be energizing, it is more useful to use models driven by *reinforcement*. Reinforcement models focus on the rewards (reinforcements) that one is getting from one's work and how these rewards energize (reinforce) continued work behavior. In a reinforcement model, then, *feeling energized by one's work is simply the experience of getting rewards directly from the work.* There is nothing mystical about it. The basic issue in this book is whether or not people are getting rewards from their work *now*.

Point 3: Intrinsic rewards are about emotions

Finally, consider how emotions are treated in the rational model. Emotions are sanitized into your "utilities" for future events. In the present moment, emotions are seen as a threat to the rationality of decision making and are therefore to be controlled. Emotions, by definition, are nonrational, and the fear is that they will lead to irrational behavior—that is, to choices that reduce future outcomes. In reinforcement models, on the other hand, emotions are at the core of motivation. Basically, *the four intrinsic rewards are those qualities of the work that feel good*—that generate positive emotions. To harness intrinsic motivation is to understand these positive emotions and to amplify them. When we get to part 4 of this book, then, we will be talking in part about how you can amplify those emotions.

How the Intrinsic Rewards Reinforce Engagement: The Energy Cycle

Figure 4 shows how the intrinsic rewards are linked to self-management.[6] Both make up an ongoing system of mutual influence— a sort of dance in which either can take the lead. The self-management events on the left provide the judgments that produce the intrinsic rewards on the right. The positive feelings involved in those intrinsic rewards, in turn, energize (reinforce) active self-management, which provides updated judgments, and so on.

This kind of system can produce upward or downward spirals. A change in either self-management or intrinsic rewards can cause this kind of shift. For example, if you interfere with some part of workers' self-management, you will tend to reduce their intrinsic rewards, which will provide less energy for self-management,

Figure 4. **The Energy Cycle**

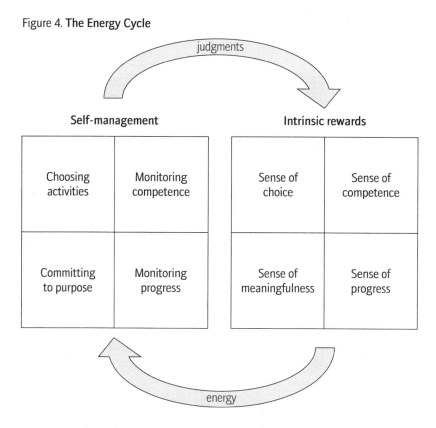

Source: Kenneth W. Thomas and Erik Jansen, "Intrinsic Motivation in the Military: Models and Strategic Importance," Technical Report NPS-SM-96-001 (Monterey, CA: Naval Postgraduate School, September 1996).

further reducing intrinsic rewards, and so on. My friends at New West like to refer to this loss of energy as an "energy leak."[7] Likewise, if you increase a worker's intrinsic rewards, you will tend to energize more self-management, which will probably lead to further increases in intrinsic rewards, and so on, until some new, higher level of engagement is reached. Again, we will be talking about how to do that in part 4 of the book.

In this system, the intrinsic rewards provide important lever-age on self-management. However, research shows that the posi-tive feelings involved in the intrinsic rewards have powerful effects on other outcomes as well. In the remainder of this chapter, we'll review what we've learned about the intrinsic rewards and their powerful effects on many of the issues you care about as a leader.

A Healthy, Sustainable Form of Motivation

Most of the research findings I'll be citing are based on a research questionnaire that Walt Tymon and I developed, now called the *Work Engagement Profile* (*WEP* for short), which is described in "The *Work Engagement Profile*" on the next page.[8] However, good work has also been done using related measures developed by Professor Gretchen Spreitzer, now at the University of Michigan, and by Professor Teresa Amabile at the Harvard Business School, so I will be citing some of their findings as well in the endnotes.

Professor Jacques Forest recently validated a French translation of the *WEP* against a number of other measures of motivation. His preliminary results, explained in "Forest's Findings About the Four Intrinsic Rewards," provide a foundation for understanding the beneficial effects of the intrinsic rewards.[9] Dr. Forest found that each of the four rewards contributes a separate positive emotion that reinforces work. People who score high on the four intrinsic rewards experience high levels of positive emotions about their work and report relatively low levels of negative emotions. He also found that their passion for work is "harmonious," in the sense that it is powered by their enjoyment of the work itself. The four intrinsic rewards are not connected to an obsessive "need" to work, a need to prove oneself to others, or forcing oneself to do things for pay. The picture that emerges, then, is of the intrinsic rewards providing a relatively "healthy" and sustainable form of

THE *WORK ENGAGEMENT PROFILE*

The *Work Engagement Profile* is the most recent iteration of a questionnaire developed to measure the four intrinsic rewards. It consists of twenty-four self-report items—six for each reward. These are examples of the items:

"My work serves a valuable purpose." (Meaningfulness)
"I feel free to select different paths or approaches in my work." (Choice)
"I am skillful in my work." (Competence)
"I have the sense that things are moving along well." (Progress)

Individuals rate their agreement with each item on a seven-point scale from "strongly disagree" to "strongly agree." The instrument is self-scoring and takes about twelve minutes to complete and score. Scores place each individual into high, medium, or low categories for each reward in comparison to the scores of others.

The *Work Engagement Profile* is printed in a twenty-page booklet with interpretive materials on each reward and its relationship to work engagement, self-management, and other outcomes. (An on line version is also scheduled for release.) Rich descriptions are provided of the experience of being high, medium, or low on each reward—to help individuals tune into their experiences of those rewards. The interpretive materials were designed with feedback from New West Institute and other users to be effective in a number of applications, including leadership training, career counseling, and organizational development.

FOREST'S FINDINGS ABOUT THE FOUR INTRINSIC REWARDS

Professor Jacques Forest of the Université du Québec à Montréal recently conducted an elaborate study of the *Work Engagement Profile* and its relationship to a number of other measures of motivation. Here is a brief summary of his findings:

- The four intrinsic rewards (sense of meaningfulness, choice, competence, and progress) are seen as four distinct feelings.
- All four rewards are accompanied by increased positive emotions about work and by decreased negative emotions.
- The four rewards tap into feelings about enjoying work activities and valuing work purposes. They do not tie into feelings about pay or protecting one's reputation.
- The four rewards measure a "harmonious" passion based on enjoying one's work, not an obsessive "need" to work.
- The four rewards correlate with three key elements of the state of "flow" during work: concentration on the work, sense of control over the work, and enjoyment of the work experience.
- The four rewards are associated with a form of commitment to one's organization that is based on liking and being proud to be part of the organization. They are not associated with two other forms of commitment involving the sense that it would be morally incorrect to leave or that one could not afford to leave.

work motivation that fulfills workers rather than a push to do things they may not enjoy. For that reason, it makes sense to think of the four rewards as the psychological "vital signs" of a healthy and engaged workforce.

Outcomes of the Intrinsic Rewards

Now, what does the research show about the effects of the intrinsic rewards?

Performance

High scores on the *WEP* show up in key aspects of active self-management, including concentration on the task and control over the task.[10] Workers who score higher on the *WEP* are rated as more effective by their managers.[11] As you would expect from the model of self-management, people who score higher on the intrinsic rewards are particularly likely to be seen as innovative—that is, to exercise their intelligence in choosing new ways of accomplishing a purpose. Research shows this to be true for both workers and managers.[12]

Professional Development

Across all organizational levels, people who score higher on the intrinsic rewards report higher satisfaction with their professional development.[13] Again, this follows from the definition of development that we offered in chapter 3—the increasing ability to self-manage. The sense that one is working on meaningful tasks, making choices, performing activities well, and actually achieving the task purpose gives workers evidence that they are developing professionally.

Job Satisfaction

A number of studies show that people who score higher on the intrinsic rewards have higher levels of job satisfaction as well.[14] In service organizations especially, job satisfaction has been shown to be a major factor in customer satisfaction and repeat business.[15]

Commitment to the Organization

Higher scores on the intrinsic rewards are also related to greater commitment to one's organization. This commitment shows up in a number of ways, including recommending the organization to friends as a great place to work and recommending the organization's products and services to potential customers.[16] In effect, then, intrinsically rewarded workers become recruiters and marketers for their organizations.

Retention

Studies show that higher scores on intrinsic rewards are related to a stronger intention to remain in the organization.[17] A study of hospitality workers found that their intent to remain on the job was much more strongly related to the intrinsic rewards than to pay.[18] Another study examined three possible reasons why people might choose to remain in their organizations: because they enjoyed working there, would feel guilty if they left, or couldn't financially afford to leave. People who scored high on the intrinsic rewards intended to stay because they enjoyed their work—not because of guilt or financial need.[19] Consider the implications of this finding for reducing turnover. As a strategy for increasing retention, wouldn't you rather have workers remain because they are intrinsically motivated and engaged rather than use financial incentives or guilt to induce people to stay who might not be as engaged?

Reduced Stress

Finally, workers who are higher on the intrinsic rewards report fewer stress symptoms.[20] A reduction of stress symptoms generally translates into lower health-care costs and absenteeism, less chance of burnout, and a generally more upbeat workforce. This finding, then, is further evidence that the intrinsic rewards are an especially healthy and sustainable source of motivation.

■ ■ ■

To sum up, research shows that the intrinsic rewards contribute to performance, job satisfaction, organizational commitment, retention, and reduced stress. This pattern of positive effects has been constant across a variety of studies by different researchers and with very different populations. We began our own research with knowledge workers: high-tech workers, engineers, research and development people, managers, and so on. Then very similar results appeared in studies with lower-paid hospitality workers.[21] Most recently, we have gotten very similar results in the developing country of India, using a wide sampling of industries, functional areas, and organization levels, as detailed in "Evidence from a Developing Country: India."[22] While the specific issues examined in each study differ somewhat, the overall pattern of results has been consistent.

■ ■ ■

So now that you've seen the effects of the intrinsic rewards, we'll get cracking on helping you build them. We'll start with the building blocks that produce the intrinsic rewards.

EVIDENCE FROM A DEVELOPING COUNTRY: INDIA

This large-scale study was just conducted in India by a team of academics from Villanova University and the Naval Postgraduate School in collaboration with the consulting firm Right Management Inc., and its Indian subsidiary India Grow Talent. The study collected information from approximately 5,000 people in twenty-eight firms across five industries: information technology, engineering/manufacturing, business process outsourcing, pharmaceuticals, and financial services. Participants in each firm, from individual contributors to vice presidents, completed the *Work Engagement Profile* along with other measures.

At the time of this writing, study data are still being analyzed. However, preliminary findings support earlier results from studies in the United States and Canada:

- Individuals recognize the four intrinsic rewards as distinct factors.
- The four intrinsic rewards are strongly related to job satisfaction.
- The rewards explain a sizable proportion of individuals' satisfaction with their organization and commitment to it—including recommending it as a place to work and speaking highly of its products and services.
- The rewards are strongly related to a sense of professional development.
- Individuals who score high on the intrinsic rewards are less likely to consider leaving the organization.

6

A Diagnostic Framework for Rewards

Now that you understand the intrinsic rewards and how they power engagement, you'll need a diagnostic framework to help you decide two things: (1) which intrinsic rewards need boosting and (2) how to boost those rewards.

We'll be using the same framework to help you manage both your own engagement and the engagement of the people who report to you. So I'll briefly introduce it to you here before we start applying it in parts III and IV of the book.

Why Do You Need a Diagnostic Framework?

The short answer is that you need a diagnostic framework to point you toward what's most likely to make a difference and to save you from having to try motivational solutions in an inefficient, hit-or-miss way.

A large number of experts have offered recommendations for energizing or engaging workers. Many of these address important pieces of the puzzle of intrinsic motivation. For example, visions are an important part of inspiration but are not the whole. Likewise, "bureaucracy busting" and delegation provide necessary freedom but are also not enough. Other writers emphasize celebrations, coaching, customer feedback, and so on.

Each of these bits of advice contains valid but partial insights about intrinsic motivation. To be sure, each bit of advice can be useful. However, each one is only likely to make a noticeable difference if it provides the missing intrinsic reward for your workers. It can be unnecessary if that motivational piece is already in place and will probably not be enough if more than one piece is missing. And, to be honest, you probably don't want to invest the time or money to try every bit of advice in a hit-or-miss way. So you need a diagnostic framework that directs you to the intrinsic reward (or rewards) that most needs attention and then to the specific building blocks that will help build that reward.

Let's look at the two steps in the diagnostic framework.

Step 1: Gauging the Strengths of the Intrinsic Rewards

If you are trying to boost engagement—whether you are "topping off your tank" or dealing with a serious deficiency—it is vital that you be able to figure out which intrinsic rewards need attention. If one or more of the people you manage have an engagement problem, for example, you will need to get beyond the judgment that they are not very engaged to figure out what is causing the problem. Meaningfulness problems, choice problems, competence problems, and progress problems are very different from each other. While difficulties with any of these four rewards can derail engagement, each will require a different sort of remedy.

So you will need some way of gauging the strength of the four intrinsic rewards. In workshops and courses, we use the *Work*

Engagement Profile we discussed in chapter 5. The *WEP* provides a score for each reward that you can compare to the scores of others who have taken the instrument. The *WEP* will tell you the relative strength of each reward and identify any that are especially in need of attention—for you and/or your team members. That is one option.[1] But there are other ways of judging the strength of the four rewards as well. In part 3 of this book, we will describe the experience of scoring high or low on each intrinsic reward to help you judge how much of each reward you are getting from your own work. Then in part 4 of the book we will talk about the kinds of preliminary signs and follow-up conversations you can have with the people you manage to help gauge their intrinsic rewards.

Step 2: Addressing the Building Blocks for a Reward

This brings us to the second part of the diagnostic framework— the *building blocks* of each reward. These are the set of conditions that allow each reward to flourish. Figure 5 lists the sets of building blocks that Walt Tymon and I culled from our research and experience and from the management literature.[2] Each set of building blocks serves as a checklist to help you troubleshoot any missing conditions that need attention for an intrinsic reward—to identify why an intrinsic reward is lower than it could be and what you need to help provide.

The next two parts of this book will discuss these building blocks in detail, along with specific actions that you can take to help provide them. As you read those parts, you will probably recognize some of the action recommendations—many have already been publicized as alleged solutions to the problems of the new work. The key value-added of this section of the book, then, is not in recommending new solutions. Rather, it is in giving you a framework that will help you choose actions that fit the needs of

Figure 5. Building Blocks for the Intrinsic Rewards

Choice:	Competence:
• **Delegated authority**—the right to make decisions • **Trust**—confidence in an individual's self-management • **Security**—no fear of punishment for experimentation and honest mistakes • **A clear purpose**—an understanding of what one is trying to accomplish • **Information**—access to relevant facts and sources	• **Knowledge**—an adequate store of insights from education and experience • **Positive feedback**—information on what is working • **Skill recognition**—due credit for one's successes • **Challenge**—demanding tasks that fit one's abilities • **High, noncomparative standards**—demanding standards that don't force rankings
Meaningfulness:	**Progress:**
• **A noncynical climate**—freedom to care deeply • **Clearly identified passions**—insight into what one cares deeply about • **An exciting vision**—a vivid picture of what can be accomplished • **Relevant task purposes**—a connection between one's work and the vision • **Whole tasks**—responsibility for an identifiable product or service	• **A collaborative climate**—coworkers who help each other succeed • **Milestones**—reference points to mark stages of accomplishment • **Celebrations**—occasions to share enjoyment of milestones • **Access to customers**—interactions with the beneficiaries of one's work • **Measurement of improvement**—a way to see if performance gets better

your particular situation. Chances are that you'll learn some new action tools, but the most important thing will be to learn when each tool can help and why.

At this point, however, you need to understand two general facts about these building blocks and actions.

It Takes More Than Job Design

One of the classic models of intrinsic motivation, by Richard Hackman and Greg Oldham, focused exclusively on aspects of job design as influences on intrinsic motivation.[3] (Their model is briefly described in resource A.) A number of the building blocks in figure 5 involve the kinds of job design factors these older models defined—fairly objective factors that can be engineered into jobs, like authority, information sources, whole tasks, and measurement and feedback mechanisms. They help enable self-management to occur and to be effective. They continue to be very important, but they are not enough!

Since that model was developed in the 1960s, a profound change has taken place in the social sciences. In this postmodern era, it is now apparent that there is only a loose connection between so-called objective events and our reactions to them. Basic ambiguities in many events allow them to be interpreted in various ways. Human behavior, we realize now, is shaped more directly by our interpretation of those events than by the events themselves.[4] So we pay a great deal more attention now to how people interpret events—to how they frame events and construct their meaning. For example, it is clear that transformational or inspirational leaders are effective because they actively shape people's interpretations of the task purpose.[5]

I invite you to think about the importance these kinds of interpretations play in your own life for a moment. If you are like me, you get a real lift from friends and family when they help you gain perspective on a discouraging event. Or consider the way that we help children learn to interpret events in a constructive way. Interpretations are so important to our motivation that you will need to address them directly—in your self-leadership and in your leadership of others.

For that reason, a number of the building blocks in figure 5 involve factors that shape workers' interpretations in rewarding ways—that make work more fulfilling and energizing. These kinds of building blocks are especially important to a sense of meaningfulness. For example, it is important for you as a leader to help workers avoid cynical interpretations of their work purpose and to create a vision of a desirable future that appeals to their passions. But interpretive factors show up in the building blocks of the other intrinsic rewards as well. Judgments of progress depend on identifying milestones, for example, and celebrations are ways of drawing attention to that progress. You can use these interpretive factors, then, to enhance or *amplify* the intrinsic rewards that workers get from self-management, providing an added motivational boost to their self-management.

Building Blocks Are Codetermined

When I started doing research on intrinsic motivation, most management writers seemed to assume that empowerment was something you did *to* workers. That seemed a little ironic since the whole point of empowerment was greater self-management and proactivity for workers. Looking back, that assumption was probably a remnant of the paternalism of the compliance era.

The reality is that workers in the new-work world play an increasingly active role in *codetermining* the building blocks in figure 5. They share information and propose their own interpretations of events. They negotiate with leaders and their teammates to initiate changes in their job designs. They are influenced by leaders, but also, in Charles Manz's phrase, exercise "self-leadership" in many ways.[6] This codetermining of the building blocks occurs between team leaders and team members all up and down the hierarchy. So some of the action recommendations will involve conversations you may want to have with your boss—as well as being open to similar conversations your team members may want to have with you.

PART THREE

Managing Your Own Engagement

$\mathcal{A}$ Management Tale, continued

THE WISE CONSULTANT told the executives what he had learned of the four Intrinsic Rewards that power workers' engagement—the sense of Meaningfulness, Choice, Competence, and Progress. He told them of the far-reaching Effects of these rewards—on Performance, Retention, Development, Commitment to their organization, and Reduced Stress. And the executives truly saw the Power of these rewards and the need to master them.

"How should we begin?" asked the executives.

"I have given this much thought," replied the consultant, "and have concluded that you must first look to Your Own Intrinsic Rewards."

The executives, who were Busy People, asked why this was necessary.

"There are Three Reasons," explained the consultant. "First, you must tune into these Rewards in Your Own Experience in order to have first-hand Knowledge of them. This Knowledge will help you to recognize and bolster the Rewards in the people you lead." Seeing wisdom in this, the executives nodded their agreement.

"The second reason," the consultant continued, "involves your Credibility. You must yourself be seen as Engaged in order to lead them for Engagement. Likewise, you must feel the Intrinsic Rewards yourself in order to help inspire them in others and to talk about the motivations you share. Without that, your efforts will not appear sincere, will not be heeded, and will breed Cynicism." Again, the executives nodded agreement.

"What is the third reason?" asked the executives.

"Ah," said the Wise Consultant, "that is my Personal Present to you, for I wish you Happiness and Long-Term Success. And learning to manage Your Own Intrinsic Rewards is a path to Sustainable Engagement and Fulfillment for you."

7

Tuning Into Your Own Intrinsic Rewards

This part of the book will help you manage your own intrinsic rewards. The present chapter will help you tune into those rewards so that you can recognize them in your own experience and make a general assessment of their strengths. Then, in chapters 8 through 11, we will cover the building blocks for each of the four rewards, with actions you can take.

How to Use This Part of the Book

Some readers will be content with their intrinsic rewards and eager to get on to part 4, which deals with leadership. If you fit that description, I still recommend that you read the material in this chapter. The descriptions of the experience of the four intrinsic rewards will also help you recognize the levels of the intrinsic rewards in your team members and allow you to talk about them more fluently.

If you are not used to thinking about your own intrinsic rewards—or if you suspect that you are not getting as much energy and fulfillment from your work as you would like—you will want to read all five chapters in this section. Mark up the pages in any way that will help you understand your engagement and what you can do to manage it.

Why Your Own Intrinsic Rewards Are Important

As the preceding installment of *A Management Tale* suggests, there are a number of reasons why managing your own intrinsic rewards will help your leadership. Understanding your own intrinsic rewards will help you recognize them in your team members. Also, keeping yourself engaged and energized will make it much easier to lead for engagement. But the point about your engagement that I most want to emphasize here is its importance to your long-term success and well-being. We are talking about your energy level and the quality of your work life.

One of the applications of this book and the *Work Engagement Profile*[1] is in management coaching and career transitions, so I have been talking to a number of people who provide that kind of coaching.[2] They treat the intrinsic rewards as psychological vital signs—as the signs that your organizational role is working for you as a person and that you are engaged and being rewarded by your work. What I hear from these coaches, however, is that a disturbing number of the managers they see are running on empty—low in intrinsic rewards and approaching burnout. I don't want this to happen to you!

What seems to happen for many of these managers is that they don't use their intrinsic rewards as a guidance mechanism—they treat them as irrelevant. Many set career goals involving extrinsic success alone or find themselves in organizations with set career paths that define success for them. Others take on new responsibilities largely out of a sense of duty or obligation. Either way, the danger is that many eventually find themselves relying on willpower alone to keep going, gutting it out with few intrinsic rewards until their energies become depleted.

Maybe a story from my own early work experience will help here. I liked college and was good at it, so I went into a doctorate program at Purdue. I wanted to excel and pushed myself pretty hard. I knew that graduate school was only temporary anyway, so I adopted a philosophy of delayed gratification. After I graduated, I told myself, I would have a real job and could then begin to enjoy life more. But—you guessed it—I applied the same self-discipline when I took my first faculty position at UCLA. The turning point came when someone told me that I didn't look very happy and asked me what I enjoyed doing. I was shocked to realize that I simply couldn't answer that question! I could come up with a long list of the things I should do or needed to do but was simply not used to thinking in terms of what I enjoyed doing. In retrospect, that was probably the beginning of my interest in intrinsic motivation. I became much better at taking stock of my own intrinsic rewards, doing what I could to build them, and incorporating them into my decisions.

Don't get me wrong. I still recognize the importance of discipline and setting goals. But I have learned that it is my intrinsic rewards that keep me energized as I pursue those goals. I have now installed an intrinsic motivation gauge on my psychological dashboard, and I pay attention to it on a regular basis. I am suggesting that you do the same. Basically, I am recommending that you learn to self-manage at the task of maintaining your own intrinsic motivation—that you commit to keeping your intrinsic rewards high, make choices to help that happen, get good at building your intrinsic rewards, and keep track of the progress you are making. Your work life is too short (or too long!) not to enjoy the adventure!

Let's get started.

Charting Your Intrinsic Rewards

If you are reading this book as part of a course or workshop, you may also be using the *Work Engagement Profile* to get a reading of your levels of the four intrinsic rewards. What I'll do here is provide a different, more intuitive way of helping you tune into those levels. I'll provide some descriptions of what it feels like to be high or low on the intrinsic rewards, and you can compare those to your own experience to get a rough notion of where you stand. Try to focus on what it generally feels like now in your job. (If you are just entering a new position or are between positions, focus in on the position you have just left.)

Meaningfulness

As we discussed in chapter 4, the sense of meaningfulness involves the opportunity you feel to pursue a worthy purpose. It's the feeling that you are on a path that is worth your time and energy—that you are on a valuable mission and that your purpose matters in the larger scheme of things.

High Sense of Meaningfulness

You know that your work—or some part of it—is especially meaningful to you when you find yourself excited about it. It's easy to concentrate on it—to focus your attention and energy. In fact, you are likely to find yourself resenting the time you spend on other, less meaningful activities and borrowing time from those so that you can devote more time to what matters. You find yourself thinking about it a great deal, and your subconscious works on it even when you are not consciously thinking about it so that you come back to it with new insights. You find that you are judging how productive of a day you had by whether or not you were able to make progress on it rather than getting sucked in by other demands on your time. You also see clear signs of your own commitment in how you manage to find ways around obstacles and how you don't take no for an answer.

Low Sense of Meaningfulness

When your work—or a part of it—is not meaningful to you, you have little emotional investment in it. You feel relatively detached and unrelated to what's going on with it. The work is empty for you. It's as though you are waiting for something else more significant to come along and are marking time or making do until it does. You may find yourself resenting the time or effort you spend on the work. You are likely to find that you avoid or delay working on it and that you are easily distracted. You may have to force yourself to keep working and your thinking may go something like this: "Okay, suck it up. You *have* to do this." If you hit a roadblock or encounter a no from a superior on a particular task, it is easy (and even a relief) to drop the task.

Charting Your Sense of Meaningfulness

Now, take a look at the meaningfulness dimension in figure 6. If you are completely honest with yourself, what does your work usually feel like? Although I've provided three reference points, you can place your mark anywhere along the line. Go with your first impression here because it is that uncensored impression that is most likely to be influencing your engagement and energy level.

Figure 6. **Charting My Own Sense of Meaningfulness**

I generally feel I am:

Wasting my time on trivial matters	Doing work that has some worth	Devoting my time to something of real value

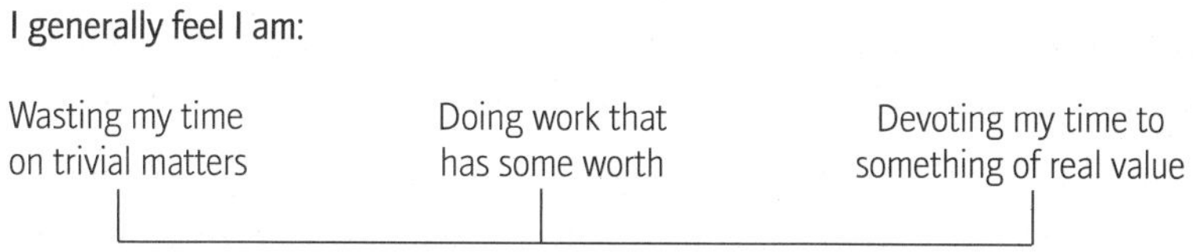

Choice

Your sense of choice is the opportunity you feel to make decisions about how best to accomplish your work purpose—to select activities (courses of action) that make sense to you and to perform them in ways that seem appropriate. It's the feeling of being free to choose—of being able to use your own judgment and act out of your own understanding.

High Sense of Choice

You know you have a sense of choice on a task when you are aware that your views and insights matter—when you need to bring your understanding and judgment to the party. If you stopped to think about it, you would find that you feel very much like an adult in these situations—with the expansive feeling of being a responsible decision maker, driving your own train. You also find that you are absorbed in understanding the task: you are curious, interested, wanting to learn, and open to information. You see visible signs of your choice in the flexibility of your behavior: you make adjustments and improvise as you see what would work better or as the situation changes. Your choices are also likely to show up in initiative, innovation, creativity, and experimentation. You also feel a strong sense of ownership of the task and feel personally responsible for the outcomes of your decisions.

Low Sense of Choice

When you feel little sense of choice, in contrast, you feel constrained and pushed by other people and forces that are driving the train. You have the sense that your own views are irrelevant so that you need to suppress them and comply. If you stopped to think about it, you would find that you don't feel much like an adult in these situations. You are likely to feel more like a younger child looking to adults or older siblings for direction. You are also likely to feel more pressure and to be more concerned about meeting others' expectations about how to do your work correctly. Your lack of choice is visible in your need to more rigidly comply with procedures and directions, with little room for initiative or creativity. Finally, you are less likely to feel personally responsible for the outcomes of your work.

Charting Your Sense of Choice

Place a mark anywhere along the line in figure 7 to indicate what your work usually feels like. Again, go with your honest first impression.

Figure 7. **Charting My Own Sense of Choice**

I generally feel I am:

Pushed and constrained	Finding some room to maneuver	Driving my own train

Competence

Your sense of competence is the accomplishment you feel in skillfully performing work activities. It's the feeling that you are doing good, high-quality work.

High Sense of Competence

You have a sense of competence when you feel that you are performing your work activities well—when you feel that your performance of those activities is meeting or exceeding your own standards. At such times, you are also likely to feel pride in the good work you are doing. If you are working on a product, such as a report, your feelings of competence may show up as a sense of craftsmanship, workmanship, or artistry. When you are dealing with other people, your feeling of competence may show up as a sense of responsiveness or deftness in handling the events and conditions you encounter. When you feel a sense of competence, you are also likely to feel a mastery of the task activities you are performing and a confidence about being able to handle them in the future. You are also likely to find yourself deeply engaged in performing the activity—paying close attention to your work as you deal with the requirements and challenges of the moment.

Low Sense of Competence

When you feel little sense of competence, in contrast, you tend to feel little pride in your performance of work activities. A low sense of competence can come in a number of forms. You may simply not care about these work activities and not be trying especially hard to do them well, taking little pride in them. You may care about these tasks but not be able to meet your standards for any number of reasons that have little to do with your ability, leaving you feeling embarrassed or dissatisfied by the quality of your work. You may find yourself dealing with challenges that are beyond the skills you have developed so far, causing you to feel overwhelmed or anxious. At the other extreme, you may have mastered your task activities so well that you are no longer challenged by them, so that you are doing the work on automatic pilot and no longer getting much satisfaction from a task that seems so easy that it's trivial.

Charting Your Sense of Competence

As you consider this intrinsic reward, it is important to remember that you are not evaluating your actual competence. Rather you are considering the extent to which you experience a sense of competence as you perform your job—how much your job gives you a feeling of competence on a regular basis. Again, go with your first impression.

Figure 8. **Charting My Own Sense of Competence**

I generally feel I am:

| Not meeting my own standards | Doing things well enough | A real craftsman at this work |

Progress

Your sense of progress is the accomplishment you feel in achieving the purpose behind your work activities. It's the feeling that your work is moving forward, that your activities are really accomplishing something.

High Sense of Progress

You have a sense of progress when you find yourself feeling encouraged about how well your purpose or objective is being achieved. You may experience this as a sense of well-being about having your plan on track and working out—a sense that you are in the midst of a successful endeavor. You are especially likely to feel in control of events at such times, as you see your activities having the impact you intended. You also have the sense that all your time and effort are paying off, so that you feel enthusiastic and eager to keep investing your time and effort in your work. If a work task is especially meaningful for you, you are also likely to feel an excitement, or even a sense of wonder, about achieving an important purpose: "Yes! It's really happening!" Your sense of progress may also involve the sense that your work is advancing quickly—that things are "really moving," that you and your team are "really cooking."

Low Sense of Progress

When you feel little progress, in contrast, you tend to feel discouraged. You are likely to feel frustrated and stuck, sensing that the purpose or objective is slipping away. Or you may feel that results are happening too slowly—that you and your team are only plodding toward your objective. You are likely to feel less effective and perhaps even a bit helpless, as events seem more outside your control. You find that it gets harder to keep up your enthusiasm and to keep exerting yourself. If this continues, you may burn out on the work eventually and see it as hopeless. Far from being energized by the work, you may begin to begrudge the effort you put into it—which now seems wasted or pointless—and to lose your commitment to it. If you remain on a task beyond this point, you may become increasingly cynical and bitter.

Charting Your Sense of Progress

Place a mark anywhere along the line in figure 9 to indicate what your work usually feels like. Again, go with your first, uncensored impression.

Figure 9. Charting My Own Sense of Progress

I generally feel I am:

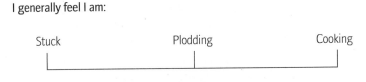

| Stuck | Plodding | Cooking |

Interpreting Your Answers

What patterns do you see in the way you charted your intrinsic rewards? There are three main regions on each chart:

- *To the left of the midpoint*—indicates fairly strong dissatisfaction with your level of that reward. This drain on your engagement and energy may make it difficult to sustain your efforts over the long haul. It's something you'll want to address.

- *From the midpoint to the three-quarters mark*—indicates a moderate or so-so level of the reward. You feel that you get some reinforcement for your efforts but less than you would like and less than what you need to be fully energized. It's enough to keep going but something that it would pay to improve.

- *To the right of the three-quarters mark*—indicates a fairly strong level of intrinsic reward. Perhaps you have some room left to top off your tank, but it's clearly enough to keep you engaged and energized.

Are there any clear differences between your ratings of the four intrinsic rewards? For example, I've found that managers in government hospitals tend to have a relatively high sense of meaningfulness because individuals' lives and health are impacted by their work, but that their sense of choice is relatively low because of the elaborate rules. Does your pattern of ratings suggest that one or more of the intrinsic rewards is more of a problem for you than the others? If so, you'll want to pay particular attention to the building blocks for that reward in the next chapters.

General Recommendations

Before we leave this chapter, here are two suggestions to help you monitor your intrinsic rewards:

- Make sure you check your four intrinsic reward levels on a regular basis. You will find that they change with different events. At a minimum, take some quiet time on weekends to reflect on them. You may also want to discuss them with a trusted friend or mentor. This is a way to build in the "intrinsic reward gauge" that I mentioned earlier. Among other advantages, that gauge will allow you to monitor your progress in building your intrinsic rewards.

- When you feel your energy surge or sag in response to work events, try to identify the specific intrinsic reward involved: "Wow, we have a chance to do something really meaningful with this project." Or "I'm discouraged by the slow progress (delays) we are encountering." Or "You know, I think I've found a better way to do this! (choice)." The better you get at recognizing these rewards as they happen, the easier it will become for you to take timely action to keep yourself (and others) engaged.

▪ ▪ ▪

Now, let's look at the building blocks for your intrinsic rewards and actions you can take.

8

Building Your Sense
of Meaningfulness

There's a lot you can do to build a sense of meaningfulness in your own job. The building blocks for meaningfulness are these:

- A noncynical climate—giving you the freedom to care deeply
- Clearly identified passions—having insight into what you care deeply about
- An exciting vision—creating a vivid picture of what you can accomplish
- Relevant task purposes—making a connection between your work and the vision
- Whole tasks—taking responsibility for an identifiable product or service

Now let's look at some actions that you can take to address these building blocks.

Creating a Noncynical Climate for Yourself

What is a cynic? A man who knows the price of everything, and the value of nothing.

OSCAR WILDE[1]

For starters, it will be important for you to control any cynicism you may have. This will be vital to your own success as a leader and also to your own intrinsic motivation at work. How do you do that? I've done research with Walt Tymon on thinking habits that influence intrinsic motivation.[2] We learned that people's thoughts are shaped by the implicit questions they ask themselves. If you size up situations by first asking yourself what's wrong, for example, you will nearly always find something that is wrong or could go wrong—and your perceptions of the world around you will be heavy in deficiencies and problems. We called this habit "deficiency focusing," and found that people who use it tend to get fewer intrinsic rewards from their work and to experience more stress.[3] This kind of thinking is a habit that can be changed. If you find that you do this, you can begin to balance your approach to situations by stopping to ask yourself what is going well and can go well. The goal here isn't to ignore problems but rather to get a more balanced view that doesn't put problems on center stage. Basically, you have to realize that this is a choice and keep choosing to see a more balanced view that includes more positives—a view that encourages hope and passion.[4]

In addition, it is also important to seek out the company of noncynical people who will help nurture your passions and ideals. This is something to look for in choosing a mentor and in picking friends and allies from among your peer group. You want people who will help you see opportunities and not those who will say, "Isn't that the pits—so typical around here."

96

Clarifying Your Own Passions

Discover what moves you.

RICHARD LEIDER[5]

In chapter 4, I invited you to think about your own passions. If a clear picture did not emerge, you have some work to do. This will be an important investment in the quality of your work life, so take some time to figure it out. It will be impossible to go after what fulfills you if you don't know what it is. Think about the times you have felt excited and fulfilled at work. What do they have in common? What dreams do you have about your ideal work? If possible, talk with supportive people in your life about this—or a coach—to get a clearer picture of your passions. You might start a personal journal to help you gain some insights. There are also a number of useful books that you can draw on for help.[6]

Once you have a clear understanding of your passions, don't keep them a secret. Share this information with your boss and people in your peer team. That way, they can help funnel "your kind" of projects or assignments to you.

One final comment here: some people are hesitant to examine their passions and dreams because they suspect that they don't fit their current job or organization. My philosophy is that it's better to find that out now and to act on it rather than staying in the job and "rusting out," to use Richard Leider's phrase.[7] You won't be doing anyone a favor in the long run—not yourself, your family and friends, or your coworkers—if you stay in a job that saps your energies. Find a team that shares your passions!

Crafting Your Own Vision

The vision needs to be lofty to capture our imagination and engage our spirit.

PETER BLOCK[8]

A vision is a big purpose—a daring and inspiring image of a future that you want to create. You need to be daring here if you want to tap your passions. Crafting a personal vision isn't the kind of short-term goal setting that encourages you to take small, obviously possible steps from where you are now. This is more about taking a longer leap into an inspiring future. What would you like your work to be like? What would deeply fulfill you or give you joy? If this vision isn't daring, it isn't likely to make much of a difference in your life. If it is daring, the excitement of that future possibility will begin to pull you forward, and you will begin finding ways to make it happen. What kind of tasks do you want to be working on? What do you want to be accomplishing and for whom? How will you recognize it when it is happening? What will your relationship with teammates look like?

Your personal vision will set an important example for team members when you begin to help your team develop its vision, and your personal vision can provide a nucleus for the team's vision. So you will want to develop your personal vision—at least in rough draft form—before you begin to talk about a vision for the team. In the same way, your personal and team visions can set an example for the higher-level peer team of which you are a member. Share these visions with your boss and peers. Serve as an advocate for a vision statement at that level that fits your personal and team visions.

Making Your Tasks More Relevant

The courage to say no. . . .
What's worth doing?

RICHARD LEIDER[9]

This building block is about the connection between the day-to-day activities you perform and your vision. Your vision won't help much if most of what you do is meaningless and saps your energy.

I have found that I need to reinvent many of my work tasks to make them meaningful. I remember a turning point early in our research when Walt Tymon and I had to make a conference presentation but had low energy levels for it. We talked about how it was time to get on with the task, and we looked at the topic to see what we "had" to do. Then, after a pause, we looked at each other and said, "Wait a minute. What could we do that would be meaningful?" Our enthusiasm reappeared, and we planned a dynamite session that got across what we felt was an important message. Since then, I routinely ask myself or my colleagues, "What could I [or we] do here that is meaningful?" when approaching a new task. That question serves to get me back in touch with my passions and vision and to identify what I want to accomplish. I invite you to use this same question.

Some tasks have little meaning, of course. You'll want to negotiate to eliminate or simplify tasks with little value. And you'll want to initiate—or volunteer for—new tasks that better fit your passions and vision. When I can, I also ration the amount of time I spend on lower-value tasks, especially during my most creative time of the day. I find that if I start the day by working on the most meaningful tasks, I have enough energy to get through some of the less meaningful tasks in the afternoon—without the feeling that I have wasted the day. From the point of view of managing your energy, then, time management is not about doing everything more efficiently. Rather it is about making sure you spend your creative time on the tasks that are the most meaningful for you.

Negotiating for Whole Tasks

Doing a job from beginning to end with a visible outcome. . . .

J. RICHARD HACKMAN AND GREG OLDHAM[10]

Having a whole task means that there is an identifiable product or area of responsibility that an individual can point to with pride. The principle of assigning whole, identifiable tasks has been applied mostly to workers rather than managers. After all, it was workers who suffered the most job simplification during the compliance era, and the recent effort has been to improve their situation. Managers' jobs have always been relatively complex.

Still, there are times when the size or wholeness of a task is an issue for managers, either individually or for task forces on which they sit. It is more meaningful to deal with a whole problem, including its causes, than to address one small part of a remedy, for example. Likewise, it is more meaningful to recommend a solution and then oversee its implementation than to simply make the recommendation. If you are going to be involved in a project, it is worth trying to make it a meaningful whole—something that you can take pride in.

Reflections

1. Do you see ways that cynicism—from yourself or others—interferes with your caring about the work you do or seeing its value? If so, how can you deal with it?

2. Do you have a clear notion of your own passions with respect to work? If not, what would be the best way for you to figure this out: conversations with others, keeping a journal, reading a book?

3. Can you articulate an inspiring vision of what you would like to accomplish at work? What would it look and feel like?

4. How can you spend more time on tasks that clearly contribute to your vision? Which unimportant tasks can be eliminated, delegated, subcontracted, or simplified?

5. Are there places in your work where you could take on a larger, more identifiable task?

9

Building Your Sense
of Choice

The building blocks for your sense of choice are these:

- Delegated authority—securing your formal right to make decisions
- Trust—having confidence in your self-management (your own confidence and your boss's confidence in you)
- Security—feeling freedom from fear of punishment for experimenting or making honest mistakes
- A clear purpose—understanding what you are trying to accomplish and being able to recognize opportunities
- Information—gaining your access to relevant facts and sources

The first three building blocks—delegated authority, trust, and security—give you the freedom to make choices. The last two building blocks—clarity of purpose and information—allow you to make informed choices.

The following are some actions you can take to provide these building blocks for yourself.

Negotiating for the Authority You Need

Control your destiny or someone else will.

JACK WELCH[1]

Once you commit to a purpose, it is extremely frustrating not to be able to use your intelligence to best achieve that purpose—to see better ways of achieving the purpose but be unable to take the right action. In effect, you hold yourself accountable for achieving the purpose but you can't control your own destiny and it eats your heart out.

The first step is to negotiate with your boss for the authority you need. In these negotiations, pay particular attention to the two concerns that your leader will most likely respond to: how the added authority would help you or your team achieve the purpose, and the ability you have shown to handle that authority. I'll discuss the first concern here and the second later in this chapter, under the heading "Earning Trust."

Do you need more authority? What specific choices do you need to make? Here, I invite you to take a moment to identify any areas where a lack of delegation is getting in the way of your effectiveness.

• Does anything slow you down and keep you from making timely responses to events—for example, waiting for decisions that you could make faster or waiting for unnecessary approvals of your proposed actions?

- Does anything limit your flexibility to meet customer needs or otherwise adapt to conditions you face—for example, inflexible rules or one-size-fits-all procedures?
- Does anything prevent you from making the most effective use of your resources—for example, not controlling your own budget or not being able to make hiring decisions?

If you answer any of these questions by describing a specific situation, then you have a case to make to your boss. Again, phrase it in terms of how it would make you or your team more effective in achieving the purpose you and your boss share.

Earning Trust

We live in a world where self-leadership—taking responsibility for knowing yourself and for engaging in deliberate and constructive thought and contribution—is increasingly a core virtue.

CLIFF HAKIM[2]

Before your boss can delegate the authority you need, you need to earn your boss's trust. Basically, you build trust by showing that you can handle that authority—that you are able to self-manage responsibly. Here, the elements of self-management provide a more detailed way of discussing your ability to self-manage: your commitment to the task purpose and your ability to make intelligent choices, to perform competently, and to make progress on the purpose. These elements also provide a way of assessing your continuing development, so you need to have candid discussions with your boss around these issues.

What if the boss agrees that you could handle the additional authority but is unwilling to delegate it to you because then it would be necessary to give it to everyone, and some of your peers couldn't handle it? Then your boss is buying into a one-size-fits-all style of delegation. Point out the importance of delegating authority based on individual or team levels of development in self-management. Suggest this as a solution to the dilemma—as a way to give you the authority you need to perform better, provide an explanation for others, and focus attention on what others could do to earn more authority.

Not Yielding to Fear

The only thing we have to fear is fear itself.

FRANKLIN D. ROOSEVELT[3]

Fear can cause people to give away their choices and power, leaving them feeling dependent on other people and events outside their influence. To be sure, there are realistic fears that need to be acted upon. But the danger is in the *unrealistic* fears that keep us from thinking clearly and acting out of our own intelligence. Psychologists tell us that some of our strongest fears are left over from childhood—when we were small and dependent, and there were scary things around that we couldn't handle. Although we are adults now, some situations can still trigger those old fears, even though we are no longer small and helpless. If we act on those fears, we wind up avoiding choices (or making bad ones), and we strengthen the power of those fears over our lives. It is useful to treat fear as a warning signal, not as truth. Examine it and talk it through with trusted friends, rediscovering your power. Then act, but out of your best thinking, not out of the fear.

Are there any fears that keep you from using your intelligence to choose new or better ways of doing your job or of making the right move to advance the task purpose? How real are those fears?

How about the fear of breaking rules? A few years ago, I had the pleasure of interviewing Admiral William Rowley, a visionary and empowering leader in naval medicine. He spoke at length on the need for people to take risks, rather than mindlessly following rules, if an organization was to excel in meeting its mission. "How about the fear of punishment?" I asked. His answer has stayed with me. He firmly believes there is no significant risk if you genuinely try to "do the right thing."[4] In cases when the rules prevent patients from getting the care they need, he pointed out, it is the bureaucrats who put patients at risk by blindly following rules who get into trouble. "Doing the right thing" stands up very well to scrutiny.

Take a moment to absorb this insight. Rules and procedures are imperfect guidelines designed to help the purpose get accomplished. When they get in the way and put the purpose at risk, you need to correct the situation by relaxing the rules or getting them changed. This is a situation where your organization *needs* you to act intelligently.

How about the fear of your boss's anger? Can you recommend changes in your boss's decisions when you are convinced he or she is wrong? Here's another military example. I recently spoke with a U.S. Marine officer who flies in large planes with sizable flight crews. As you know, the marines have a strong respect for rank and authority. Nevertheless, it is vital that subordinates on the flight crew be able to assertively point out problems to the pilot during flight if they are to save lives. I learned that crew members receive training to be able to make assertions like "It is my duty to you and our plane to tell you when something will hurt us" and then to give specific information.

Again, take a moment to try on similar words for dealing with your boss. You have a *duty* to your boss, as well as to the organization and your task purpose, to point out dangers. Notice that this approach appeals to the mutual concern you and your boss have for the task purpose. Notice also that this approach avoids the issue of whether the boss's decision was right or wrong. Win-lose arguments about whether past decisions were right or wrong are pointless and destructive, like arguments over blame. This marine's approach is to give his boss new information that he believes is important to the boss and is likely to lead to a new understanding and decision. It works when you sincerely have the task purpose at heart and when you can also listen to your boss's information in return. (I'll get back to this collaborative approach in chapter 11.)

Finally, consider the worst case. You have been negotiating with your boss but cannot get the authority you need and have earned. You are also trying to do the right thing but getting punished for it. Then keep in mind that you do have other choices beyond this job—you can look for a transfer within the organization or for another organization where you could use your judgment in the service of a meaningful purpose. After all, this is a new labor market where organizations compete on their ability to attract and keep self-managing people. If your experience is typical in this organization, you won't be the only good person to leave. Why would you want to stay?

Clarifying Your Purpose (and Seizing Opportunities)

People like you and me may become giants. Giants see opportunity where others see trouble.

MAX DEPREE[5]

Making intelligent decisions requires a relatively clear purpose. Yet in the new-work world, you are likely to encounter more and more ambiguity. Your delegated tasks are likely to be stated in more general ways to give you the flexibility to handle unexpected events. And the pace of change is increasing so you will be bumping into more unexpected situations that weren't planned for—that aren't clearly covered by your purpose. This ambiguity means that you will need to keep clarifying and reinventing your purpose as you meet these new circumstances. Looked at another way, change presents you with opportunities to advance your vision in new ways. If you can think of it this way, change becomes a sort of Easter egg hunt where you try to spot and seize these opportunities—rather than an avalanche that threatens to bury you in debris.

Take a moment to think about any changes you are facing at work. What opportunities are there that you could get excited about? What specific purposes could you take on to capitalize on these opportunities?

To be sure, you will need to coordinate with your boss as you spot these opportunities. But don't be shy here. The organization needs you to take initiative in this area. *You* are the person on the scene—the organization's advance party. You are the best person to seize on these opportunities and to find ways to harness them to your unit's purpose.

Getting the Information You Need

Information about business strategy, processes, events, and business results . . .

EDWARD LAWLER[6]

Let me describe an old compliance-era dilemma. Many command-and-control bosses didn't want their people bothering people outside their function and required all questions to go through them. So subordinates asked their bosses a few, select questions but limited them so they wouldn't seem pesky or stupid. Feeling that they were somehow supposed to know these answers, they were forced to make many guesses and then to wait rather anxiously to hear how well they had guessed.

Luckily, the new information rules are quite different in most organizations. Hierarchies are flatter, and contacts across departments are encouraged. The norms now call for people to talk to whoever has the information they need to make sound decisions. That requires establishing direct contact with people in other functions and often with people at different organizational levels in those functions. Increasingly, it means going outside the organization to get information from customers and suppliers. It also means having access to computerized networks and databases that link people throughout an organization and often between organizations.

So take a moment to ask yourself if there are still some areas where you are guessing because you don't have access to information you need. If so, what would you need? An improved information system? A better database? Introductions to a few people? How can you help make this happen?

Reflections

1. What additional authority might you need to better accomplish your work? Can you make a good case to your boss about how this would help your unit's performance?

2. Are there times when your boss doesn't seem to trust your ability to self-manage enough to give you the freedom you need to make decisions? What kinds of discussions could you learn to have with your boss to reassure her or him?

3. Are any fears keeping you from "doing the right thing" to advance your purpose? How realistic are they?

4. Are there opportunities that you haven't yet recognized in the unexpected events or changes you encounter in your work? Are there ways you can use them to advance your purpose? Do you need to reinvent or further clarify your purpose to handle these situations?

5. What information would help you make better decisions and how can you get it?

10

Building Your Sense of Competence

As a manager, some of your sense of competence will come from how competently your team performs its activities. Here, I'll concentrate more on the sense of competence you get from performing your own activities well.

The building blocks for your sense of competence are these:

- Knowledge—possessing an adequate store of insights from your education and experience
- Positive feedback—receiving information on what you are doing well
- Skill recognition—getting (and giving yourself) due credit for your successes
- Challenge—executing adequately demanding tasks that fit your abilities
- High, noncomparative standards—using standards that don't force rankings or comparisons between yourself and others

The following are some actions that will help you acquire more of these building blocks.

Getting the Knowledge You Need

All men who have turned out worth anything have had the chief hand in their own education.

SIR WALTER SCOTT[1]

Much of your learning will come from your own experimentation and the feedback you receive. Remember the feedback arrows in the self-management model in chapter 3? Feedback can lead you to improve the way you perform activities or to choose new activities that will result in better performance. But it would be very inefficient to limit yourself to this type of direct learning. You'll want to find out what other experts have learned and see how it will help you. New knowledge can give you new options that would take you a long time to discover for yourself.

Although it may be difficult to find the time to seek out this knowledge, this is a high-leverage path for increasing your own sense of competence. Take the courses you need, read books and articles, and find your own experts. The quality movement taught us the value of benchmarking high-performance organizations and learning their lessons. Do the same for individuals whose competence you respect—either peers or superiors. If it's a peer, buy lunch for the two of you and encourage a knowledge exchange, which may develop into a friendship. If it's a superior, try out a mentoring relationship. Either way, there will be rewards for the experts you've chosen as well as for you. Your interest will serve as a form of recognition for them, and sharing their learnings will amplify their own sense of competence. So—once again—don't be shy here.

Getting the Feedback You Need (and Listening)

The need to know and the fear of knowing. . . .

ABRAHAM MASLOW[2]

There may be areas where you'll need to ask for feedback on your activities. If running meetings is an important part of your job, for example, you may want to begin holding brief postmortems after each meeting to get feedback on the meeting. You may also be able to bring in consultants or other coaches to provide feedback on some of your activities.

However, it is likely that you already get a fair amount of feedback directly from many activities. You get many clues to tell you if you are explaining your ideas well to a team member, for example, or if you are handling negotiations with a customer well. In most cases, you also receive suggestions from the people who depend on you. If most of the building blocks are in place, your team members will care about the competence of their work and about their task purposes, so they will let you know what you can do differently to help.

In many ways, competence depends on listening to this feedback—even though, as the quote that opens this section suggests, everyone feels ambivalent about getting evaluative feedback. The importance of the feedback is obvious: it contains information you need to improve your competence. My friend and colleague Barry Leskin likes to say, "When you're in trouble, the facts are friendly." A book by Janelle Barlow and Claus Moller, *A Complaint Is a Gift*, conveys a similar message about listening to feedback from customers.[3] Accepting valid feedback is also part of your integrity—and it encourages honesty in your team members. If you suppress feedback or don't act on it, your team members will eventually stop telling you the truth, and that can lead to disasters. In an extensive study of significant management failures, Dartmouth professor Sydney Finkelstein tracked each failure to top executives who cut themselves off from this sort of honest feedback.[4]

Still, getting negative feedback can hurt. Try to focus on the fact that the feedback is about helping your performance. If, on the other hand, the feedback given within your team does seem to be especially negative and hurtful, it's probably time for some team training on constructive, appreciate feedback.

It will also pay to take responsibility for giving yourself appreciative feedback. When you can, take a moment after an activity—especially an important or especially difficult one—to give yourself some recognition. Again, look out for deficiency focusing. For those of you who *are* deficiency focusers, I'll share some personal history here. Years ago, before I started doing research on the topic, I realized that I had a built-in assumption that I "should" be problem solving whenever possible—scanning for difficulties or shortcomings and figuring out how to deal with them. This kind of thinking had become a strong habit—and one that often left me anxious and dissatisfied. It occurred to me rather suddenly at one point that my assumption was the problem! So I began very deliberately to spend more time noticing what was working well and celebrating it—even though it felt uncomfortable at first. That change in thought patterns has made a surprising difference in my intrinsic motivation and in the general quality of my life. If you are a deficiency focuser, increasing your sense of competence may be as simple as giving yourself permission to enjoy your good work and then putting that decision into practice. Catch yourself doing well!

Recognizing Your Own Skill

You see, you can't please everyone,
So you've got to please yourself.

RICK NELSON[5]

If you are fortunate, you'll receive recognition from team members, your boss, and others. When this happens, my advice is simple: *let it in!* Look out for the "Yeah, but—" reflex. "Yeah, that went well, but I almost dropped the ball." Or, "Yeah, I pulled that off, but let's see how I handle tomorrow's meeting." That reflex is a way of negating the recognition and your own sense of competence. If you find you do this, try practicing phrases like, "Thank you. That did go well, didn't it?"

Still, it's impressive how often the word *thankless* is applied to many tasks. Clearly, you can't always depend on others' recognition. You'll need to recognize your own skill. Here again, look out for any tendency you may have to exaggerate the importance of factors other than your skill—luck, others' help, or an easy task. Don't short yourself here. Recognizing your competence is important to your intrinsic motivation and also allows you to confidently take on the kinds of challenges you can handle.

Managing Challenge in Your Own Work

One must learn to balance the opportunities for action with the skills one possesses.

MIHALY CSIKSZENTMIHALYI[6]

The trick here is knowing how and when to say no—and when to take on more challenge. When your plate is full or you are unable

115

to meet your own standards, you have to be able to resist additional assignments. (Chapter 11 will discuss collaborative approaches to these negotiations.) The alternative is to stretch yourself so thin that you violate your own standards in order to simply get it done—or else burn yourself out trying to do it all. When you face such a request, one approach is to lay out your current projects and your standards so that the other person understands how the request would affect your performance.

On the other hand, if everything is running smoothly, you are in danger of losing interest. Then it's probably time to take on something more challenging. This may mean some new initiative in the team or an additional special project you take on in your peer work team. It also means beginning to talk with your boss about advancement possibilities that will keep you challenged.

Setting High, Noncomparative Standards for Yourself

This above all: to thine own self be true,
And it must follow, as the night the day,
Thou canst not then be false to any man.

SHAKESPEARE[7]

It's important for leaders to hold themselves to high standards. The quote is from *Hamlet* and tells us something about the foundation of all our standards for ourselves. In that play, old Polonius has been trying to impart some wisdom to his son Laertes, who is about to leave home. Polonius does this by trying to share some of the standards of conduct that he has learned. This last piece of advice is the central core of his wisdom—the importance of integrity and honesty. The quote illustrates several important truths.

First, it's hard to talk about standards, and especially leadership standards, without discussing issues of character. Good leadership—like good work of any kind—is not about cutting corners, doing what is expedient, or going for flash or form instead of substance. Good leadership and good work in general is what works over the long term, what meets the test, and what stands up to close examination. Your character is shaped by the degree to which you ask yourself these same demanding questions. Ultimately, your sense of competence comes from being deeply honest with yourself. This self-honesty is the core of most moral codes and systems of ethics. You are the judge for your own sense of competence—and one who is hard to fool for very long! So good work usually involves some soul-searching about whether your actions are right in your own eyes. It's about being able to look at yourself in the mirror and stand tall. This is the essence of "to thine own self be true."

Polonius is also saying that, if his son is honest with himself, he'll soon discover the importance of being honest with others. Again, interpersonal honesty and integrity is a foundation principle of interpersonal conduct in virtually all moral systems. It is especially important in the new leadership role, where effectiveness means having credibility with workers who are more free to say no. For this reason, a number of recent books about leadership focus on character, credibility, and integrity.

The quote suggests one final truth. Polonius comes across as a bit of a windbag in the play, and his son is less than enthusiastic about listening to his father's wisdom. People, it seems, need to internalize their own standards of conduct as they find them relevant to their own experiences. You simply can't transmit these kinds of standards in lists. People have to be looking for them to recognize their usefulness and to translate them into their own circumstances.

If you are a leader, what does all this mean about clarifying your own leadership standards? It means that you need to keep asking yourself the important questions until you have clear standards that fit you and your circumstances. You can read a number of good books to suggest these standards. But you have to find the standards that fit. So keep taking the time to ask yourself the hard questions and to update your answers. What standards do you really use now to judge your leadership? What really are the most important ways that you can add value through your leadership activities? What would it look like to be doing them well?

As you ask yourself these questions, try to avoid the trap of competitively ranking yourself with respect to other managers. That sort of ranking creates winners and losers. You don't want to start resenting others' competencies or minimizing their competence to feel better about your own. As a leader, you want to be able to encourage competence in all the people around you without being threatened by it. Celebrate others' excellence, learn from it, and contribute to it.

Reflections

1. What knowledge would most help you do your work better, and how could you get it—from mentors, coaches, experts, books, courses, or other sources?

2. What feedback on your activities would be most helpful in terms of building your competencies? Is there anything that is interfering with your ability to listen to and take in constructive feedback? Do you and the people around you know how to give appreciative feedback?

3. How good are you at giving yourself credit for your successes? How good are you at accepting compliments about what you have done well? What can you do to improve at this?

4. Is your work challenging enough to demand your full creativity and attention but also matched to your skills? If not, what changes could you make?

5. In your heart of hearts, what standards do you apply to evaluate your leadership? Can you keep asking yourself how you might best add value as a leader? Can you celebrate the excellence of the people around you without resentment?

11

Building Your Sense of Progress

The building blocks for your sense of progress are these:

- A collaborative climate—working with people who help each other succeed
- Milestones—using reference points to mark your stages of accomplishment
- Celebrations—finding occasions to enjoy your attainment of milestones
- Access to customers—interacting with the beneficiaries of your work
- Measurement of improvement—knowing when your performance is getting better

The following are some actions you can take to help develop these building blocks.

Building Collaborative Relationships

Think win/win; seek first to understand, then to be understood; synergize.

STEPHEN COVEY[1]

In collaborative relationships, people look for solutions that meet everyone's concerns when disagreements or conflicts arise—that is, they look for win-win outcomes. (A model of collaboration and the alternative approaches to conflict is covered in chapter 17.) It is especially important to have a collaborative relationship with your boss so you are able to have open, problem-solving discussions about important issues. However, you will also want to build these kinds of relationships with peers, your direct reports, and clients. I invite you to think for a minute about any noncollaborative work relationships you may have that are interfering with your own task progress. As you do this, try to avoid issues of blame and to see these relationships as opportunities to hone your collaborative skills. I'll offer a few how-to suggestions here that have proven helpful for me.

First, I suggest that you announce your wish to make the relationship more collaborative and, without blame, invite the other person to join you in trying to make it happen. This sort of invitation can mark an important transition point in a relationship. Without this step, any change in behavior from you may mystify the other person or even look like a trick. What you're really doing here is trying to create new expectations about how to handle the work issues that come up in your relationship. Be prepared to explain how collaboration might help both your task purposes.

Then you'll need to begin with the nuts and bolts of the collaborative process. Ask if this is a good time—and agree on another specific time to meet if you can't go ahead right now.

At that meeting, you'll need to confront the conflict issue—to start talking about it. (If you don't do this, you're avoiding it.) The important objective here is to begin this discussion by trying to understand both sets of underlying concerns involved in the conflict. Use active listening to understand the other person's concerns. Mirror back what you are hearing until the other person agrees that you understand. Then try to state your own underlying concern until the other person understands it. You will find that it will be easier to listen to the other person's concerns when you know that yours will be listened to as well. Likewise, many people find it easier to state their own concerns when they know that it won't be at the other's expense.

Once you both understand each other's underlying concerns, you'll need to pose the conflict as a mutual problem: "Is there some way that we can satisfy your concern for x and my concern for y?" As you offer your ideas and invite the other person's ideas, it will pay to keep an open mind and to be flexible about new solutions. Don't make the mistake of getting locked into a competitive argument over solutions: "We should do x." "No, we should do y." The trick is to keep focused on your underlying concerns and to welcome any course of action that would satisfy them. In the negotiating literature, Dean Pruitt describes this stance as "firm flexibility"—being firm about satisfying your concerns but flexible about solutions.[2]

As your behaviors in a relationship become more collaborative, you'll find that the relationship changes in other ways as well. Since collaboration is high in both assertiveness and cooperativeness, you'll build both respect and liking for each other and create a foundation for trust. This will make it progressively easier to handle future issues in a collaborative way—to help you both make progress together. For more information about when and how to collaborate, see my booklet, *Introduction to Conflict Management*.[3]

Developing Your Own Milestones

Mark milestones publicly: Post timelines and encourage people
to color in their progress.

TERRENCE DEAL AND M. K. KEY[4]

Milestones are the way we mark progress on a lengthy task. They
are the visible signs of movement toward our purpose that make
our progress tangible. Without them, we may know intellectually
that we are moving forward on a task but don't get the kind of
convincing evidence of progress that we need to stay energized,
so projects can seem to drag. Stop a minute to think about where
your team has come from and where it is headed. Do you have a
clear idea of the stages involved in your vision for the team, and
how to recognize them when they occur? Are you tracking those
signs so you can recognize progress? Or consider a more specific
project you are involved with. When was the last time you experienced a real sense of progress on that project?

It is easy to feel progress at dramatic transition points on a
task—when groundbreaking occurs for a construction project,
when a first draft of a report is completed, and so on. The rest of
the time, you may need a more detailed route map of the project
stages and substages to recognize that progress is occurring. Make
sure that you take the time to identify those stages and to chart
your accomplishment of each stage. On long stretches of repetitive work, you may need to create your own milestones to mark
progress. When I do a swim workout, for example, I count laps and
pay special attention when I reach a quarter of my target distance,
the halfway mark, and the three-quarters mark. Those are psychologically significant points, and they help keep my energy level up.
Why not figure out when your project is approximately a quarter
completed, half completed, and three-quarters completed?

Taking Time to Celebrate

Celebrate . . . the small wins.

TOM PETERS[5]

Celebrations are energizing ways of immersing yourself and others in a shared sense of progress. There are lots of ways of celebrating, and I'm going to assume that you can think of several. So rather than write about how to celebrate, I'm going to try to counter some of the concerns that prevent people from celebrating. See if any of these statements sound familiar to you.

- Concern #1: "It's childish"—As I write this, I have come to terms with the fact that part of me *is* still a child. The trick is to restate *childish* as *childlike*. Psychologists tell us that we carry our earlier developmental stages with us as we mature. The childlike part of us is the part that gets enthusiastic and excited—an important core of our energy. So from a motivational point of view, the last thing you want to do is to suppress that childlike source of energy. A better goal is to integrate it with your adult reasoning—to find ways of building that enthusiasm and harnessing it to the tasks that you care about. So why not give yourself permission to celebrate a little—to keep your energy and passion alive?
- Concern #2: "If I slow down, I may stop"—There's a kind of all-or-none reasoning connected with this concern: either I run full-out or I stop, so I'd better keep running hard. But even runners need to pace themselves. If they don't, they tire and burn out. You're in this for the long haul, so pace yourself and take an occasional breather. Think of celebrations as investments and renewals and as insurance against burnout.

- Concern #3: "I don't want to brag"—Some people are concerned about appearing prideful or provoking jealousy or resentment. But bragging is about how cool *you* are, while celebrating is about moving forward on a task. There's an important difference. If this is a concern for you, look for ways of celebrating modestly. Keep the task in the foreground. You can celebrate your good fortune if you like, which acknowledges that there was some luck involved. You can also reduce jealously by sharing your celebration with team-mates who shared in the task and with friends and family who genuinely care about you.

Making Contact with Customers

Nonsales employees are energized by the opportunity to serve customers directly.

BOB NELSON[6]

This quotation is from Bob Nelson's book, *One Thousand and One Ways to Energize Employees*. It is based on the experience of a shoe company that trains all its employees to be able to fill in for the sales staff in taking orders from customers. In his book, he also talks about a melt-shop operator in a steel products company who was given the opportunity to travel with two salespeople.[7] In both cases, meeting the customers gave people a chance to see what a difference they were making for their downstream customers.

Stop for a moment to consider which of your customers are most important to you and your personal vision. Who would most lift your spirits by contacting you to let you know that you are making a real difference for them? This is often a complex question. Sometimes it's a group of end users far removed from you, sometimes an internal customer, a direct external customer, or your boss. And many leaders think of their team members as their most important customers.

Now, are there any of those important customer groups that you don't personally interact with? Or, if you interact with them, are there some with whom you don't discuss the differences you make for them? If so, how could you meet with these people and get the evidence you need to find out that your work makes a difference?

Measuring Improvements (and Tracking Intrinsic Motivation)

Anything worth doing is worth measuring.

PRINCIPLE USED BY WHOLE FOODS[8]

Measuring improvements is important for a sense of progress on any long-term task. However, it is often difficult for leaders. Leadership is a relatively unstructured task in the sense that it isn't a simple, repetitive cycle of activities. So it is difficult to measure improvements in leadership very directly. I think of leadership as a matter of doing whatever is needed to help a team identify and achieve purposes, meet quality standards, and keep team members motivated. What this means is that measuring the value-added of leadership boils down to measuring improvements in a team's achievement of task purposes, its work quality, and its motivation.

Notice that I've listed improvements in team members' motivation as one of three key measures of leadership. That is a logical conclusion from the premise of this book—that intrinsic motivation plays a key role in today's work. So if you are a leader and buy that premise, you'll want to keep tracking the intrinsic motivation of the people under your leadership. How else will you know whether they are energized by their work tasks, and what elements of intrinsic motivation still have room for improvement?

Reflections

1. Are there any noncollaborative work relationships that interfere with your progress? What can you do to initiate a change in those relationships?

2. Does any major part of your work seem to be dragging because you don't have milestones to measure your progress against? If so, can you take time to reflect on where you began and how far you've come? Can you identify milestones you have already met and lay out future ones to help you recognize the progress you are making?

3. Has anything been keeping you from celebrating the progress that you have been making? Why not resolve to celebrate it now?

4. What kinds of conversations or experiences would help you learn about the positive difference you are making for the people you want to benefit from your work?

5. Are there measurements that you could collect to better help you recognize improvements in the performance and motivation of your work team?

PART FOUR

Leading for Engagement

$\mathcal{A}$ Management Tale, concluded

THE EXECUTIVES ATTENDED to their own Intrinsic Rewards—their sense of Meaningfulness, Choice, Competence, and Progress. They saw the Power of these rewards in their Engagement—and how the Building Blocks for the Rewards shaped their Energy for work.

The executives more Fully Understood what they had only vaguely suspected about their Energy and Engagement. And they vowed to Use these ideas to better monitor and build their Energy. For some executives, the ideas were truly a Revelation—a new Doorway into Energy and Fulfillment. And, looking through that Doorway, they had a new glimpse of What Work Could Be—for themselves and others.

■ ■ ■

However, it was now time to speak of Leading for Engagement—for that was why the executives had come to the Wise Consultant.

"You will find," said the consultant, "that your employees are Very Much Like Yourselves in their need for Intrinsic Rewards. Remember this and you will avoid foolish mistakes. Just as your Energy ebbs and surges, so too does theirs—so that Leading for Engagement is an Ongoing Task. You cannot 'fix' Engagement and then move on to other things." The executives saw the truth of this and nodded.

"Truly," said the consultant, "Leading for Engagement is the very Core of managing. Do you recall what Engagement is in today's work—Active Self-Management?" The executives nodded. "Then

I can state my message in one sentence. *To Lead for Engagement is to Enable people to Self-Manage—but also to Seek and Amplify the Evidence of Meaningfulness, Choice, Competence, and Progress that keeps them Engaged.*"

Seeing that this was important, the executives asked the consultant to say more.

"When you approach work tasks with your employees," said the consultant, "focus the conversation on the steps of Self-Management—on pursuing what is Meaningful, discovering the Choices they have, doing things Competently, and assessing the Progress being made. And Listen to their Needs, that you may better enable them in these steps." The executives nodded their understanding.

"But remember this also, for it is Truly Important: To be Energized and Stay Engaged, your people will need Credible Evidence of the Meaningfulness, Choice, Competence, and Progress involved in their work. For, as we have seen, it is these Intrinsic Rewards that Power Engagement. Empty Slogans and Facile Assurances will not be enough for them—just as they would not satisfy you. Part of your Leadership is to Seek Evidence of these things that may not be obvious to them and to Share it with your people—especially for any Reward that is low."

"And how will we know which Rewards are low?" asked the executives.

"Ah," said the consultant, "you can Measure them to be certain. But if you speak regularly and honestly with your people about these things—and if you listen well—they Will Tell You what is missing for them. And that is So Much Better than guessing."

12

General Tips on Leading for Engagement

This part of the book will help you build the intrinsic rewards that power engagement in the people who report to you. This chapter provides some general tips. Chapter 13 will help you chart the intrinsic rewards in your team to set priorities for change. Chapters 14–17 will give you detailed suggestions for building the intrinsic rewards in your work team. Then chapter 18 will offer a brief summary and a final piece of advice.

So, let's get to the general tips.

Focus on the Steps of Self-Management

Part of leadership is focusing attention—and the conversation[1]—on what matters most. To lead for engagement you will need to make sure that people are asking the questions that are central to self-management:

- What can we do here that is most *meaningful* in terms of our broader purpose?
- What *choices* do we have? Can we find a creative way of doing this?

- How can we do this in a *competent* or high-quality manner?
- How can we tell if we are making *progress*—actually accomplishing our purpose?

Model that behavior for your team by focusing team discussions on those issues, featuring them in your written communications with team members, and raising those issues in conversations with individual team members.

An important skill here is learning to frame specific situations in terms of these four issues. For example, if team meetings bog down for some reason, resist the urge to vent frustration or assign blame. Mention that this situation is *slowing progress* toward attaining your team's purposes. With that in mind, point out that holding productive meetings is an important *competence* area for the team to work on. Devote attention to skill building in that area— for yourself and team members.

Play a Positive Role

In chapter 5 we discussed the energy cycle, in which employees' self-management requires them to make judgments of meaningfulness, choice, competence, and progress—which then reinforce and energize the employees' continued self-management. Leading for engagement is about taking positive actions that push that cycle to higher levels.

In his later years, quality advocate W. Edwards Deming emphasized intrinsic motivation, which he often referred to as "pride of workmanship" or "joy in work."[2] However, his writing focused on what leaders commonly did wrong that stifled intrinsic motivation. Most of his motivational advice, then, was about what *not* to do—for example, not managing by fear, quotas, or inappropriate reward systems. Some of the building blocks in this book deal with the points Deming covered, but I have recast them in terms of a more positive role. Rather than focusing on not pushing the system downward, it seems more useful to think of your role as finding ways to keep pushing it upward—to get beyond not being a negative influence and instead work at being a continuous positive influence.

Figure 10 provides a shorthand way of thinking about this positive leadership role. It's based on feedback I gave to an organization that was having trouble developing self-management in some of its work teams. This particular organization used the "coaching" metaphor, so I tried to expand on that idea. "Coaching" was a little too vague to capture the key elements of leadership that were needed. At its core, coaching has to do with helping players build their skill or competence of performance. This is an important part of the leadership role, as the figure shows. But in reality, good coaches, like other good leaders, do much more to develop and motivate players. So I used three more sports terms to draw attention to other parts of leadership that were often neglected in this organization. Some supervisors acting as coaches were micromanagers who continued to use command-and-control tactics, so I pointed out that "handing off" is what allows workers to develop choice. Good coaches also have a tradition of inspiring people— building meaningfulness by focusing attention on an important purpose. Finally, good coaches keep players energized and developing by keeping score on measures of progress and by cheering or celebrating that progress when it occurs. *Coaching* on its own addresses only the competence aspect of work, but taken together with *handing off*, *inspiring*, and *keeping score and cheering*, it provides a pretty good overview of the positive leadership that can help you develop and engage workers.

Figure 10. The Positive Role of Leadership

Leading for **Choice:** **Handing Off**	Leading for **Competence:** **Coaching**
Leading for **Meaningfulness:** **Inspiring**	Leading for **Progress:** **Scorekeeping and Cheering**

Listen and Enable

Part of your positive leadership involves enabling people to self-manage. Use your conversations with people to encourage self-management toward your unit's purpose—but also to listen. If you listen well, these conversations will give you information about obstacles that are interfering with self-management—silly rules, lack of cooperation from other departments, insufficient resources, and so on. With that information, you can take action to remove the obstacle and create conditions that better enable your people to be effective.

As a side note, these conversations will also give you clues to any intrinsic rewards that need attention. We will be discussing those clues in more detail in chapter 13.

Provide Credible Evidence of Meaningfulness, Choice, Competence, and Progress

Another part of your positive leadership role involves providing evidence that boosts intrinsic rewards. Your team members will get some of these intrinsic rewards directly from their work. But to move self-management to a higher level—and to accelerate that movement—look for opportunities to amplify those intrinsic rewards. You can do this by finding and sharing credible evidence of the meaningfulness, choice, competence, and progress present for your team.

You can use many different types of evidence. You can provide *explanations*—like why the current project is especially meaningful in the larger scheme of things. You can collect *data*—for example, on increasing customer satisfaction with your unit's services. You can tell memorable *stories*—for example, about how people have found creative ways of accomplishing tasks. You can *reframe* events—such as focusing on how quickly the unit's performance is improving toward a new standard rather than the fact that it is not quite there yet. And you can use *demonstration projects* to show what is possible for your team and to generate a sense of momentum.

Your credibility is crucial in this part of leadership.[3] Empty slogans, posters, and unsubstantiated assurances aren't enough in this era of overmarketing and "spin." It is important that your evidence have the ring of truth and that your message be sincere. And, once again, it is important that your messages be consistent. I've learned from interviews that people will be watching intently for consistency in what you say and especially for consistency between your words and your actions.

Here are two examples that show how judgments of consistency shape confidence in a leader's credibility. The first involved

Admiral William Rowley, whom I mentioned in chapter 9. Early in his term as commanding officer, the units in the hospital responded to his leadership by painting their work areas, which gave the entire hospital a rapid symbol of progress. Even the emergency room personnel, who were contract employees from another organization, caught this spirit and began painting their spaces. But their staff headquarters, which was more parental and control oriented, ordered them to stop painting "because they might fall off the ladders." Rather than squash their initiative, Rowley came in over the weekend and finished the job himself. Compare that story with one from an Army Reserve unit, where the commander emphasized the high importance of a weekend drill but didn't show up himself because of a skiing event. Both stories were told to me repeatedly by people in the two organizations. One story cemented a leader's credibility, while the other basically destroyed it.

Explain Your Leadership Philosophy

Make sure that people understand your managerial philosophy around self-management and intrinsic rewards so that they know what is behind your actions and can incorporate it into their own thinking. A clear philosophy is especially important for higher-level leaders who are trying to create a culture of engagement within their part of the organization. If you fit that description, consider building this content into the training of supervisors and managers in your unit. You will also want to keep explaining it and reminding people of this philosophy. Changing a culture is an ongoing task, not a one-time event, so, again, consistency of message is vital.

Here's another example involving Admiral William Rowley, who had been recommended to me as an innovative and empowering

138

leader in naval medicine. When I interviewed him, he had just taken a naval hospital that was "chugging along" at a normal pace and turned it into a hotbed of innovation and excellence.[4] Rowley had been especially articulate about his leadership philosophy and found daily opportunities to share it and to tell stories that supported it. Some of the points he used with his staff are shown in figure 11. Feel free to adapt them to fit your situation or to develop your own phrases.

Figure 11. **One Leader's Words**

On Choice:	**On Competence:**
• Take risks, be innovative • Control your own destiny • Do the right thing • Remove fear and blame • Remove artificial barriers • Give people all the resources • Share information	• Convey confidence (in self and others) • Emphasize that there is something powerful about people • Give positive feedback • Recognize people • Expect more of people than they do themselves
On Meaningfulness:	**On Progress:**

• Do something more
• Make the world a better place
• Do the right thing
  – for patients
  – for the hospital
• Give the parent organization "more than it deserves" (excellence rather than simply a fair exchange)
	• Show we are on the move
	• Demonstrate things are happening
	• Remind everyone anything is possible
	• Show people what's possible (through demonstration projects)
	• Give progress reports

Source: Interviews conducted with ADM William Rowley, USN.

Engage the "Motivational Middle"

My friend Bruce Vincent at the New West Institute[5] finds it helpful to talk about the three levels of engagement a leader is likely to encounter in a work group:

- Committed members—already highly engaged and intrinsically motivated
- Compliant members—doing what's required but more dependent on extrinsic rewards and authority
- Complacent members—disengaged and often complaining to other group members

It is tempting for leaders to play favorites with the committed members of the team by interacting more frequently with them, forming an "inner circle" or "in-group" with them, and treating others as an "out-group." But research shows that this treatment further alienates the out-group members and further reduces their intrinsic rewards.[6]

As Vincent points out, a more effective strategy is to focus on engaging the compliant members, who are often the largest of the three groups. An engaged middle group, together with the already-engaged committed members, will form a large enough majority to support a culture of engagement in the group. Among other advantages, this culture will leave the complacent members with no audience for their complaints and leave them with the choice of either "getting with the program" or moving on.

Engaging the motivational middle doesn't mean ignoring the other groups. What it does mean is aiming your message—and your evidence—at the level of that group: "We've been doing an acceptable job, but now we've got a real opportunity to do something we can be proud of," "Look what we're capable of," and so on.

De-emphasize Money as a Motivator

As you move intrinsic rewards into the foreground in your conversations with team members, be sure to move money into the background as a motivational issue. I've put a more detailed treatment of the role of money in resource B, "Putting Money in Perspective." Here, I'll cover some of the high points of this issue.

Remember that you want people to become highly motivated by the intrinsic rewards they get from active self-management. As you achieve that goal, pay systems will have less and less impact on day-to-day motivation so the last thing you want to do is to keep reminding people about the rewards of the pay system. When people work mostly for the pay, they tend to do only what is rewarded. They also tend to game the system and do the work only well enough to earn the dollar rewards. In contrast, people who are working for intrinsic rewards do what is needed, whether it involves monetary compensation or not. They perform to their own high standards— even when no one is looking. And they adapt their behavior to fit new circumstances that the pay system couldn't anticipate.

My advice is to treat pay mostly as a matter of fairness. People want fair pay for their performance and will become unhappy if they feel they are being treated unfairly. So try to resolve any issues of unfairness affecting pay before they become demotivators.

The pay system will still be there as a backup for any people who remain compliant or complacent, of course. But it would be a mistake to assume that your people are motivated extrinsically, treat them accordingly, and thereby strengthen that motivation.

■　■　■

Now, let's get to the specifics. Chapter 13 will help you get started by charting your first impressions of the average level of intrinsic rewards in your team and setting priorities for improvement.

Reflections

1. Think of a current or past management situation that concerned you. Practice framing that situation in a way that focuses on meaningfulness, choice, competence, and progress.

2. Are there any tendencies that keep you from playing the positive leadership role discussed in this chapter: inspiring, handing off, coaching, and keeping score or cheering? If so, how can you counteract those tendencies?

3. How easy is it for you to listen to the needs of your team members? If this is an issue, how can you improve?

4. What evidence could you share with your team members right now to build their sense of meaningfulness, choice, competence, and progress?

5. Is there anything that holds you back from endorsing the leadership philosophy in this book? If so, can you modify it so that you can articulate a philosophy that you can sincerely and consistently share with your team members?

6. What is your impression of the composition of your team in terms of committed, compliant, and complacent members? Are you addressing the motivation of the "motivational middle"?

7. In your conversations with team members, are you putting pay in the background as a fairness issue rather than a motivator?

13

First Impressions
and Priorities

This chapter will help you develop an initial strategy for raising the engagement level of your team. We'll begin by helping you form initial impressions of the levels of the four intrinsic rewards in your team. Then we'll talk about a general strategy for building engagement.

First Impressions of the Intrinsic Reward Levels

If you want a precise measure of your team's sense of meaningfulness, choice, competence, and progress, consider using the *Work Engagement Profile*[1] described in chapter 5. The *WEP* will allow you and the team members to see how their scores compare to those of other people who have taken the instrument. That process can be an engaging kickoff to a more detailed discussion of intrinsic motivation in your team.

What I'll try to do here, however, is to give you an alternative method—a less precise, more general way of gauging the levels of those intrinsic rewards. I'll point out some common signs to help you recognize high and low levels of each reward. If you then follow up with more detailed conversations with team members, you will get a fair sense of those levels before you begin to set priorities for improvement.

As you think about your team members, keep in mind that they will likely vary in their degree of engagement, as we discussed in the last chapter. So try to focus on the people in the "motivational middle" of your team—the average members.

Recognizing a Sense of Meaningfulness

When team members have a high sense of meaningfulness, they care strongly about their work purpose and will generally be persistent and assertive in attempting to overcome obstacles. They will try to advance the purpose even when it isn't rewarded and no one is looking. If they experience problems that they cannot handle themselves, they are likely to assertively press for some change to remedy the problem. In leading for engagement, then, you need to expect spirited conversations with your team members about how to best accomplish the work. Chapter 17 will talk about collaborative ways of channeling this energy when disagreements arise. But the last behavior you want to encourage is passive acceptance of the status quo, general complaints that aren't directed at solutions, or doing only what's rewarded. Those are signals of a low sense of meaningfulness—and evidence that you will need to dig deeper to tap into people's passions.

At the team level, however, there is another layer of complexity regarding meaningfulness of purpose. You want commitment to a *common* purpose. When your team has a strong shared sense of purpose, you will find high levels of cooperation in the service of the purpose, with people helping each other advance their portions of the work. If you find that people are strongly committed to *different versions* of the work purpose, in contrast, you are likely to encounter different factions pushing their versions of what's meaningful—and less cooperation. Here, the challenge in leading for engagement is to arrive at a shared version of the purpose—one that incorporates the passions of different factions into a larger, more complete view of the purpose.

So take a moment to reflect on your first impression. (See figure 12.)

How high is your team's sense of meaningfulness with respect to a common, shared purpose?

Now, realizing that this is only your first impression and that you can collect more information through conversations with team members, chart your team by placing a mark anywhere along the line below.

Figure 12. **Charting My Team's Shared Sense of Meaningfulness**

My team's shared sense of meaningfulness:

Low   Moderate   High

Recognizing a Sense of Choice

When team members have a high sense of choice, they feel free to use their intelligence in the service of their purpose. The reality is that they are most likely to actually exercise that choice when their purpose is highly meaningful. Then team members' sense of choice will show up in *initiative*[2]—taking required actions and trying to get buy-in from others on new projects and procedures.

Their choices are also likely to be *innovative*, as each team member applies his or her intelligence to finding the best way of doing something, rather than simply complying with old procedures. They are also likely to *experiment* with new ways of doing their tasks in order to learn what works best. Finally, team members are likely to feel ownership of their tasks and to feel responsible for the outcomes of their choices.

When meaningfulness is strong but choice is low, your team members will feel less free to use initiative but will bring you *suggestions* or *proposals* for new ways of doing things—often lobbying assertively for them as discussed above. These actions, then, are evidence that your team's sense of choice is somewhat restricted.

Sense of choice may be harder to judge when team members' sense of meaningfulness is low. Then team members will have less reason to show the initiative, innovation, experimentation, or assertiveness that would allow you to recognize their sense of choice. While they might feel they have the ability to choose, that ability may remain unused. You may have to talk with them to learn about their sense of choice.

How high does your team's sense of choice appear to be?

Again, chart your team by placing a mark anywhere along the line below.

Figure 13. Charting My Team's Sense of Choice

My team's sense of choice:

Low   Moderate   High

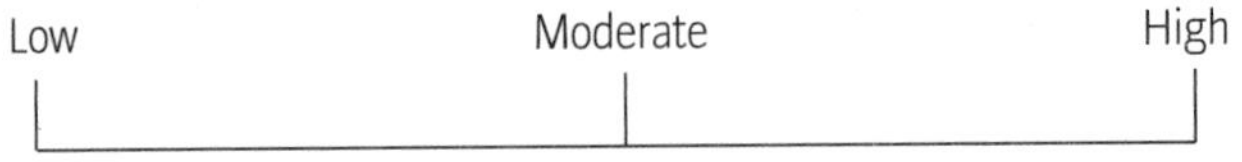

Recognizing a Sense of Competence

If your team members share a meaningful purpose with you and see you as helping them better accomplish that purpose, they will be more likely to bring up performance problems they are having and seek your coaching. That will give you much of the information you need to judge their overall sense of competence, as well as identify areas of competence that may need development.

A high sense of competence will show up as pride in one's work. Team members are likely to point out examples of their work or ask you to observe them in action. They are also likely to display confidence when taking on new work that is related to what they've been doing.

In contrast, a low sense of competence usually shows up as embarrassment and dissatisfaction with work quality. Team members may also be hesitant to take on new work. Because there are different causes, a number of other signs may help you understand the source of the problem. People may feel overwhelmed by too much work or by too much that is new. They may feel unprepared—because of insufficient training or experience. Or they may feel awkward because they haven't yet mastered the skills they are learning. Some may even be bored by skills that now come so easily that they no longer feel any challenge or sense of competence from applying them.

How high does your team's sense of competence appear to be?

Again, chart your team by placing a mark along the line below.

Figure 14. Charting My Team's Sense of Competence

My team's sense of competence:

Recognizing a Sense of Progress

A sense of progress comes from the final step in the self-management process—making sure that the team is actually moving forward in accomplishing its purpose. In many ways, then, this intrinsic reward represents your team's bottom-line judgment of its own effectiveness and success. It is a key part of team morale.

A high sense of progress is likely to show up as pride of accomplishment, enthusiasm that plans are working out, and the feeling that team members are part of a successful venture. Team members are likely to feel a sense of momentum—that they are "on the move" or "really going places." If the team's purpose has a high level of meaningfulness, then team members will also be excited that the purpose is being realized—that they are actually achieving something important through their efforts. A high sense of progress will also serve to validate the team's choices and competence and further serve to build team cohesiveness. Among other things, a high sense of progress is likely to be reflected in greater team confidence in your leadership and your management philosophy.

In contrast, a low sense of progress shows up in the feeling that the team is dragging, in a rut, stuck, or actually losing ground in some way. If the team is committed to a meaningful purpose, there will also be real frustration and discouragement from not being able to advance their purpose—and perhaps the feeling that their purpose is slipping away. A low sense of progress will often lead the team to question its collective judgment and competence and to undermine team cohesiveness—sometimes with a need to assign blame. As leader, you may get more than a little of this blame, as the team is likely to feel that part of your responsibility is to ensure that the team is effective.

How high does your team's sense of progress seem to be?

Again, rate your team by placing a mark along the line below.

Figure 15. Charting My Team's Sense of Progress

My team's sense of progress:

Interpreting Your Ratings

What patterns do you see in the way you charted your team's intrinsic rewards? Just as in the figures in chapter 7, there are three main regions on each chart:

- To the left of the midpoint—indicates that you are fairly strongly dissatisfied with the level of that reward in your team. This drain on engagement and energy may make it difficult for the team to sustain its self-management efforts over the long haul. It's something you'll want to address as a leader.
- From the midpoint to the three-quarters mark—indicates a moderate or so-so level of the reward. Your team receives some reinforcement for its efforts, but less than it would like

and less than the team will need to be fully energized and engaged. It's enough to keep the team going, but something that it would pay to improve.

- To the right of the three-quarters mark—indicates a fairly strong level of intrinsic reward. Perhaps the team has some room left to make improvements, but it's clearly enough to keep the team engaged and energized.

Here are two important aspects of your team's ratings to look at:

- *Average score*—If you averaged your team's four ratings, which of those three regions would it fall into? What does that tell you about how strongly you believe your team is already engaged and intrinsically motivated? Looked at another way, how much would you need to change in order to create a strong culture of active self-management in your team? Is this a matter of a few refinements and touch-ups, or would it take a systematic change effort for you and the team?
- *Outlying scores*—Are some of the scores markedly different from the others? For example, are meaningfulness and competence high, but choice and progress low? If so, you have an idea of where the major problems lie—and where you should concentrate your efforts. You will still want to talk with team members to verify your impressions, but these low scores will give you some initial topics to begin asking about.

Setting Priorities

Let's nail down some priorities for an action plan.

- *If your ratings of intrinsic rewards are high*—Congratulations to you and your team! I suggest that you talk with team members to verify the accuracy of your ratings. You'll also want to read the next four chapters to get new ideas for touch-ups and to ensure that you are able to keep team members highly engaged.

- *If some ratings are high and others are lower*—You will also want to talk with team members to verify your ratings. And I still suggest that you read all four of the following chapters. But you will clearly want to focus first on building those intrinsic rewards that are lower than the others.

- *If your ratings of intrinsic rewards are mostly moderate*—This is a common pattern in teams that are getting the work done but without fully tapping into members' intrinsic motivation. Again, you'll want to talk with team members to verify your ratings. And you'll want to read all four of the next chapters on building the four rewards. But here is some important advice about priorities among the four intrinsic rewards: give highest initial priority to the sense of meaningfulness—getting commitment to a shared, meaningful purpose. Wanting to achieve that purpose will provide a rationale for the team to take the rest of the self-management process seriously. Next you will need to make sure that people have the building blocks for choice and competence—to be able to actively pursue the purpose. Then it will be important to find ways of building the team's sense of progress—to show the team that they are on the move and that their self-management efforts are being successful.

- *If your ratings of intrinsic rewards are mostly low*— This pattern suggests that your team members may be disengaged or complacent, and your leadership situation may be more challenging. Again, you'll want to talk with team members to verify your impressions. You'll also want to see if there is any dramatic event in the team's recent history—for example, a past disappointment or a continuing grievance or conflict—that would help you explain the low intrinsic motivation. You'll want to be aware of any such underlying issue—and try to address it—before you start trying to lead the team for engagement. The good news is that if your ratings are correct, chances are that the team members aren't enjoying the current conditions and would welcome an improvement—as long as they see that you are sincere and have a plan. At any rate, you won't want to leave the team in this condition. So read the next four chapters and follow the same sequence of priorities discussed in the preceding paragraph.

■ ■ ■

Next we turn to the practical suggestions for building each intrinsic reward in your team, beginning with a sense of *meaningfulness*.

Reflections

1. How would you summarize your pattern of ratings for your team's sense of meaningfulness, choice, competence, and progress?
2. How can you make sure that your ratings are accurate?
3. If your ratings turn out to be accurate, what priorities should you set for building the four intrinsic rewards?

14

Leading for
Meaningfulness

This chapter will guide you in building a sense of meaningfulness in your team. As we discussed in chapters 2 and 3, it is the pull of a meaningful work purpose that initiates the rest of the self-management process. So ensuring a sense of meaningfulness is often a key place to begin leading for engagement.

The material in this chapter is organized around the five key building blocks of meaningfulness:

- A noncynical climate
- Clearly identified passions
- An exciting vision
- Relevant task purposes
- Whole tasks

Each of these building blocks, when missing, will create an obstacle to meaningfulness. You can use this set of building blocks as a diagnostic tool to troubleshoot the sources of low meaningfulness in your team and then use the suggested actions to create those missing building blocks.

Building a Noncynical Climate

Some people get their kicks stompin' on a dream....

SINATRA[1]

It is very difficult for a work group to get energized around a meaningful purpose if the members don't feel safe to talk about their passions. One of the greatest joys of group work is a shared excitement about what is possible. But one or two vocal cynics can be enough to stifle the excitement.

Consider what cynicism is about. Cynical comments are aimed at embarrassing or shaming people who express idealism and passion. Instead of people being energized and rewarded by their passions, cynicism serves to punish and suppress those passions—the opposite of what you want to happen. It is important that the leader counter these voices in group discussions and help to establish group norms that encourage idealism and passion.

How do you do that? Peter Block spells it out well in his book *Stewardship*.[2] The power of cynics, according to Block, is that they have facts to support their position. There *have* been idealistic purposes that didn't pan out in the past and passions that were disappointed. So it doesn't make sense to argue that the cynics are wrong. You can acknowledge those past disappointments and empathize with them. But you also need to point out that cynicism and passion are choices that people make. You can announce your own decision to strive to accomplish something of value. And you can invite others to join you, including the cynics. Once the remaining members of the group see the choice, it will be hard for them to say, "Yes, cynicism is a great choice; let's work without hope and passion."

Clearly Identifying Passions

There is a longing in each of us to invest in things that matter.

PETER BLOCK[3]

The team needs to identify its shared passions for a number of reasons. Identifying passions moves them (and the associated intrinsic rewards) to the foreground of the team's thinking about motivation. Otherwise, team members may be thinking they are mostly there for the money, although most will recognize that the work is sometimes fulfilling. You can remind people that all the team members could be doing other jobs to earn a living but have chosen to do this work. What is it that team members care about? Without the clarity created by identifying and naming passions, a sense of meaningfulness is a mysterious, hit-or-miss experience at work. Once the team understands the contents of its passions, it can pursue meaningfulness in a more systematic way: "Aha, that's what we care about. Now let's go after it." Finally, understanding its shared passions is a powerful unifying force for a team. Teammates are likely to think more highly of each other and to treat each other as allies in pursuit of a common purpose.

Note that this building block is not about getting the team to endorse any top-down mission statement. Nor is it about trying to sell your own passions to the rest of the team. If you are to harness the passions of the team, you want to start by learning what those passions are. So you will need to talk with your team members, one on one, about what they care most deeply about in the work. As you do this, you will probably find that some workers won't be able to answer very directly. Some younger workers may just be discovering that they have passions for their work, and others will know that they have passions but won't be able to label them very well. But most will be able to give you examples of times when they have been most excited or cared most about their work. You can suggest words that help them pinpoint their passions until you both get a handle on them.

As you have these conversations, you will likely find that many workers have settled for work that does not fulfill their passions because they haven't believed that fulfilling work is possible. To get at their passions, you might talk with them about their *dreams*. Dreams are not low-level, practical, or compromised purposes. They are more audacious and more directly related to passions. You will be able to feel the difference in tone, energy level, and even posture when people's conversations get into the vicinity of their passions and dreams. It is a powerful reminder of the energy and potential fulfillment involved.

After you have talked with your team members, you can identify the largest areas of overlap in the team's passions. I suggest you share your findings with the group as a whole to get their reactions. But be aware that once this happens and the group begins to talk openly about its passions, group members will want some significant action to pursue those passions. You and the team will need to follow through in some significant way, or you will be creating more cynicism.

Providing an Exciting Vision

If you don't know what the end result is supposed to look like, you can't get there.

VINCE LOMBARDI[4]

A vision is a big purpose for the team—a macro-image of a future that the team wants to create. It crystallizes the team's passions into an audacious and exciting possibility that captures the team's imagination. It is a shared, realizable dream that team members can harness their efforts to achieve. Without this shared vision, the team's passions lack a focus or target and can be dissipated in different, uncoordinated directions.

As the leader, you can get lots of input from the team for this vision. But stating the vision and backing it up are ultimately your responsibility. Leadership researchers James Kouzes and Barry Posner found that teams' strongest needs from their leaders were a vision for the team and personal integrity in its pursuit.[5] As we discussed in the previous chapter, consistency is important here. Developing a vision is not a one-time, check-the-box requirement. Leaders need to keep stating the vision and backing it up with action.

What does a good vision look like? It must speak to the team's shared passions. In a technical service unit within an organization, for example, shared passions may involve creating cutting-edge technological innovation and helping clients. A good vision statement for that unit might involve becoming a *recognized leader in technical innovation* with *delighted clients*. But such a simple statement is not enough. A more complete and concrete picture needs to be painted of what this would look like. For example: the team would hold a number of patents, be benchmarked by similar units in other organizations, and be invited to professional conferences to speak on its innovations. Likewise, the team would get high-satisfaction ratings from its clients, receive many referrals from current clients, and receive many unsolicited testimonials for its work. These details make the vision more real and compelling for team members. Equally important, they will later provide ways of recognizing progress toward attaining the vision.

Ensuring Relevant Task Purposes

I want to get to a point where people challenge their bosses every day. Why do you require me to do these wasteful things?

JACK WELCH[6]

While a vision is a big purpose for the team, team members' day-to-day work is made up of smaller, more concrete tasks—making things, ordering supplies, filling out reports, attending meetings, and so on. It isn't enough to have an exciting vision if many of these micro work tasks remain mundane or pointless. To energize one's work, it is important that these day-to-day tasks clearly contribute to the vision. Otherwise the drag of the mundane tasks saps the energy provided by the relevant ones.

The team's vision, then, provides a rationale for redesigning and pruning the tasks performed by team members. Busywork tasks that do not clearly contribute (often called "B.S." by workers) need to be eliminated. Necessary housekeeping tasks with little value-added for the vision can be subcontracted where possible or at least simplified. The goal is to free more time to devote to realizing the vision. Part of your job as leader is to buffer the team from low-return demands. Among other things, this means negotiating with superiors and other departments to reduce paperwork requirements—and making sure that you call meetings only for important issues and run them efficiently.

Enlist your team members to play a major role in this work redesign. The excitement of the vision can provide the necessary energy. Under the leadership of Jack Welch, General Electric had great successes in bottom-up redesign through its "Workout" process.[7] I have seen the energy and creativity that emerges from this process when people realize that their bosses will actually listen to their recommendations for eliminating pointless procedures. This can happen in your group. Redesign doesn't have to be imposed on workers. If workers are committed to a meaningful purpose, they will initiate changes to remove obstacles to its accomplishment.

Providing Whole Tasks

Completion of a whole and identifiable piece of work. . . . It is more meaningful to assemble a complete toaster than to solder electrical connections on toaster after toaster.

J. RICHARD HACKMAN AND GREG OLDHAM[8]

Finally, it is important that work tasks be designed or allocated so that individual workers are given whole projects where possible, or at least major, identifiable portions of a project. This established principle of job design allows workers to make a larger, more identifiable contribution. It also provides workers a larger potential source of pride. In thinking about this building block, I find it useful to imagine workers bringing their children to work and trying to answer the question, "What do you do?" If the answer is a long list of miscellaneous little tasks, it is hard to imagine the children (or their parent) feeling much pride. So it is helpful to give service workers responsibility for all services required by a given set of clients, and to give a staff member responsibility for an entire report (rather than collecting data for some of it).

■ ■ ■

Next, we will look at building your team's sense of *choice*.

Reflections

1. Is there a significant amount of cynicism in your team that inhibits discussions of what people truly care about? If so, how can you counter it?

2. Do you, and the team, have a clear understanding of team members' shared passions? If not, what can you do to make them explicit?

3. Do you have a clear vision for your team—a big purpose that would embody the team's shared passions? If not, how can you and the team begin to put one together?

4. How many of your team members' regular activities are experienced as relatively mundane or pointless, sapping their energy? Are there ways that you can eliminate or simplify these tasks, so that team members can spend more time on tasks directly related to the team's purpose?

5. Do the members of your work team have "whole" tasks so that they can feel ownership of a complete task and take pride in its accomplishment? If not, what changes could you make?

15

Leading for Choice

This chapter will help you build a sense of choice in your team. As we discussed in chapter 3, exercising intelligent choice is a primary way that workers add value in today's work—adapting their behavior to the requirements of different conditions and coming up with innovative solutions to the problems they encounter. So ensuring a sense of choice is a vital part of your leadership for engagement.

Of the four intrinsic rewards, leaders have the most control over workers' sense of choice. Leadership style is often described by the amount of choice given workers—from autocratic (little choice) to participative or delegative (much choice).[1] Likewise, advocates of job enrichment or worker empowerment have emphasized the importance of the leader's delegation of authority to workers. Still, this delegation is not always a simple matter. And delegating authority is only one step in creating a genuine sense of choice.

There are five building blocks of choice:

- Delegated authority
- Trust in workers
- Security (no punishment for honest mistakes)
- Clear purpose
- Information

Delegated Authority

Power to act and make decisions about the work in all of its aspects.

EDWARD LAWLER[2]

Delegation gives a worker the formal right (authority) to make decisions within whatever limits are spelled out. Management books often make delegation sound like a clean, unilateral action by the leader. Actually, delegation is often a messy, interactive process and is sometimes the result of workers' pressuring for more choice. It involves negotiations and discussions that need to take into account the workers' abilities to self-manage.

Here, I need to discuss the leadership trap of *micromanagement*— a trap that many well-intentioned leaders fall into. The mechanisms of the trap work something like this. You would like to delegate more authority to workers, and you decide that you will do this as soon as the workers show they can handle it. In the meantime, you feel the need to closely manage and control events, making most of the operational decisions. What you are less aware of is that this micromanagement—even if you intend it to be temporary—often prevents the workers from being able to self-manage or otherwise show that they could handle more authority. So workers continue to act in a dependent way, and you are trapped into an exhausting attempt to make all the decisions while wondering why workers aren't as responsible as you are.

What's the way around this trap? I conducted a study with two colleagues, Susan Hocevar and Gail Fann Thomas, in an organization that had implemented worker self-management.[3] Where groups were having trouble becoming self-managing, sure enough, we found that leaders felt conflicted and stuck over being able to let go: they knew they were supposed to delegate, but didn't feel their teams were ready. In contrast, where workers had made the change more successfully, we found leaders who saw their job in terms of *developing* workers. Even though workers weren't fully ready, these managers committed to the development of self-management in their teams and then began to delegate enough authority for them to grow into. These managers discussed delegation, team development, and self-management quite openly with the teams. They reached agreement on the team's current level of self-management, gave the team a manageable level of increased authority that took some stretching to cope with, helped team members develop the self-management skills to handle it, and then kept repeating these steps.

Demonstrating Trust

If you put fences around people, you get sheep.
Give people the room they need.

JAMES COLLINS AND JERRY PORRAS, CITING A 3M PHRASE[4]

Once you delegate, it's important that you not hover nearby, waiting to grab the reins again if needed. I've spoken with leaders and teams that are caught in a yo-yo-like cycle of delegation, reclaimed authority, redelegation, and so on. Team members in this situation realize that the choices are not really theirs and keep looking over their shoulder to see when the boss will step in. It's a matter of trust. To experience choice, the team needs to trust that you will keep your word and give them the room to make decisions, and you need to trust them enough to do so.

Trust also means removing unnecessary rules and controls that prevent team members from using their judgment. To do this, it is useful to shift the questions you ask yourself in evaluating rules and controls. Rather than asking the conservative question "How do I know I should remove this rule [or control]?" a more appropriate question is, "Is there any obvious value-added that prevents me from *eliminating* this rule [or control]?" General Electric, for example, reduced unnecessary approvals by teaching the following principle: if you haven't made a significant number of rejections, stop requiring team members to get your approval.[5]

Another sign of trust is delegating significant decisions. Although it is important to delegate decisions that individuals will be able to manage, it is usually a mistake to begin by delegating the safest, relatively trivial ones. Remember the importance of meaningfulness in self-management? Your team members are likely to see the delegation of trivial decisions as a sign of low trust and to learn that self-management is not very meaningful.

Finally, it is a good idea to express your trust out loud by actively encouraging team members to take on new responsibilities. This is especially important for workers who have been micromanaged for long periods and are concerned about taking this new risk. When you delegate significant authority, then, it is useful to tell team members why you have the confidence to give them that authority. David McNally has discussed this sort of encouragement by using the metaphor of young birds testing their wings and learning to fly. His message is reflected in the title of his book *Even Eagles Need a Push.*[6]

Providing Security
(and Allowing Honest Mistakes)

Drive out fear.

W. EDWARDS DEMING[7]

A sense of choice requires that workers feel safe to make what appear to be the right decisions—to experiment, adapt, and innovate. Recall that this sort of problem solving is one of the main advantages of self-management. Allowing innovation, in turn, means that some mistakes will happen. As leader, you should do what you can to reduce unnecessary mistakes by matching how much you delegate to your judgment of team members' abilities. You can also keep informed and be available to help them (without retaking control) if they need your help. But you cannot avoid all mistakes if you want the benefits of self-management and intrinsic motivation. When workers try out new solutions, for example, their experimentation necessarily involves some trial-*and-error* learning.

Progress and learning, then, mean expecting and allowing some honest mistakes—and using them as important learning opportunities. If workers are afraid of being punished for honest mistakes, they are likely to play it safe and stay very close to well-established, tried-and-true solutions. Team members will be afraid to trust their judgment and work will become less about doing the tasks in the best possible ways and more about not getting in trouble. When that happens, you are back to a conservative conformity, despite your delegation of authority.

Here lies a trap that some leaders and entire organizations fall into. In the military, it's called a "zero-defects mentality." To be sure, there are a few tasks—nuclear power safety, for example—where mistakes can be catastrophic. On those tasks it is important to be vigilant for possible errors and to take a hard line with workers who allow them to occur. The trap is in extending this policy of vigilance and punishment to tasks where mistakes are not catastrophic. When that happens, prevention of mistakes gets treated as a more important measure of effectiveness than making progress on the task purpose. What follows is an intolerance of mistakes that cascades down the organization. Leaders whose own jobs are on the line threaten their team members with punishment for mistakes. In their vigilance for finding mistakes, leaders are more likely to be seen as "playing gotcha" than supporting the team. Besides conformity, the common symptoms of the zero-defects trap are withholding information on mistakes, falsifying records, and a preoccupation with assigning blame.

The remedy, of course, is to actively support team members' rights to make intelligent mistakes. Honest mistakes, mistakes that made sense given the information at hand, need to be treated as *good* mistakes and used to produce learning. In *Thriving On Chaos*, management consultant Tom Peters described a number of well-run organizations where the value of speed and innovation was so well recognized that the organizations actually had awards for intelligent mistakes.[8] In organizations that do not have this philosophy, defending good mistakes by team members may take more courage on your part. You may have to take the heat for those mistakes, defending them on the basis that they were risks worth taking and that they resulted in significant learning.

Providing a Clear Purpose

Alice went on. . . . "Would you tell me, which way I ought to go from here?"
"That depends a good deal on where you want to get to," said the Cat.
LEWIS G. CARROLL[9]

The first three building blocks—delegation, trust, and security—give workers the freedom to make choices. But freedom alone won't allow workers to make effective and rewarding choices. The two remaining building blocks—clarity of purpose and information—allow workers to make informed choices. Without these factors, choice can become anxious guesswork, providing more stress than satisfaction.

I have already discussed the importance that purpose has to a sense of meaningfulness. The point here is that a clear purpose is also needed to enable choice—as the quote from *Alice in Wonderland* suggests. That is, team members need to understand what defines success on a task before they can decide what path to take to get there. As leader, then, you need to make sure that you and your team members share the same understanding of long-term purposes and more intermediate task goals, without your getting too far into the weeds about how to meet those goals.

Providing Information

People without information cannot act responsibly.

KEN BLANCHARD, JOHN CARLOS, AND ALAN RANDOLPH[10]

If team members are to make good choices—and to get satisfaction from making those choices—they need access to all sorts of relevant information: technical information, customer information, upcoming changes, and so on. So as you delegate more and more decisions, you will find yourself thinking less about what *you* need to know about those matters and thinking more about what your team members need to know. You will shift significantly from the role of decision maker to the support role of ensuring that your team members are informed. At G.E. under Jack Welch, the principle was to push decisions down to the lowest level where ability and information exist, and then to ask pointedly, "If they don't have the information, why not?"[11]

As a leader, you generally have a wider range of contacts outside the unit and more access to strategic information from upper management than your team members have. You will need to relay useful bits of information from these contacts to your team, of course. (You'll also find yourself responding to information requests from your team.) But as you delegate more, you'll also want to make sure that your team members get wired into their own networks so they can get the information they need more directly and quickly—or else you'll become an information bottleneck. This means helping them get on line access to relevant accounting, customer, or other databases, as well as getting introductions from you into the informal network of relationships that may be helpful for their decision making.

■ ■ ■

Next, we will look at building your team's sense of *competence*.

Reflections

1. Have you delegated enough authority to your team members to allow them to self-manage? Have you avoided the micro-management trap? Do you see your role in terms of further developing your people's capacity to self-manage? Are you comfortable discussing your team members' development with them as a basis for deciding how much self-management they should have?

2. Do you trust your team members enough not to hover over them waiting for mistakes? Are there rules or controls that you could eliminate to require fewer approvals before they act? Do some team members require a bit of a push to take on more authority?

3. Are your team members afraid to make intelligent mistakes? Do you recognize the need to allow some intelligent mistakes as the price of experimentation, learning, and development? Have you avoided the "zero-defects" trap? Is there anything more you can do to support intelligent risk taking in your team?

4. Do your team members have a clear enough understanding of their purpose and goals to make informed choices? If not, how could you help provide more clarity?

5. Do your team members have enough information to make informed choices? If not, what kinds of facts, documents, data-bases, and personal introductions do they need in order to get the information they need?

16

Leading for Competence

This chapter will guide you in building a sense of competence in your team. As discussed in chapter 3, a sense of competence comes from the third step in the self-management process, monitoring one's work activities for quality of performance. So a sense of competence is directly related to performing work activities well—another important way that engaged workers add value.

There are five building blocks for competence:

- Knowledge
- Positive feedback
- Skill recognition
- Challenge
- High, noncomparative standards

Providing Knowledge

Management Principle #6: Institute training on the job.

W. EDWARDS DEMING[1]

Over time, workers gain a great deal of knowledge through their own experiences with tasks—through experimentation and feedback. Some of this knowledge is implicit or *tacit*—difficult to express, like how to perform a physical skill gracefully. The rest is *explicit* knowledge that can be expressed and shared. This explicit knowledge includes learnings about techniques, best practices, and rules of thumb that contribute to competent performance. Adding to this knowledge can be a relatively quick way of increasing competence, allowing workers to jump ahead of where they would otherwise be on their own learning curve.

As a leader, you'll probably need to provide some of this knowledge through relevant training courses, so you should check to see what's available. But you'll probably also want to harvest and transfer some of the knowledge that already exists in your team or elsewhere in the organization. A variety of techniques are now available for bringing knowledge to the surface and sharing it in this age of learning organizations. However, the basic idea is to help team members get in contact with others who have developed some competence in the same or related tasks. What can they learn from each other and from you? Who else outside your team, or even outside your organization, is a resource?

Providing Appreciative Feedback

The worst mistake a boss can make is not to say well done.

JOHN ASHCROFT (BRITISH EXECUTIVE)[2]

Workers must be able to monitor the competence of their ongoing activities in order to make adjustments in their performance. Much of this feedback is available to workers as they work with a product or customer, but some needs to be measured more elaborately. Under self-management, workers must be given the tools and data needed to assess the quality of their performance and to make adjustments themselves whenever possible.

Even so, there are likely to be some aspects of performance that are hard to assess and adjust without help. This is the reason we need coaches to help us improve our tennis, for example. There are aspects of my tennis serve that I simply cannot see well and that a coach can see more easily. So, as leader, you will often be able to provide helpful coaching to team members. As you provide this coaching, keep in mind that the psychology of coaching is quite different from the micromanagement of the compliance era. If the other building blocks are in place, workers will care about the competence of their work, will feel that they are in charge of their performance of activities, and will be responsible for their own competence. In that context, you are available as a resource to offer observations that may help them.

As you give feedback, it is important to be aware of the dangers of deficiency focusing—discussed in chapter 8. In a given situation, you can choose to focus on the positives or the negatives, for there will usually be both. Hearing that 99 percent of his or her work is done well is experienced differently by a team member than hearing that 1 percent of his or her work is substandard, even though both statements may be true. It is clear from the research done by Edward Deci and his colleagues that positive feedback increases the sense of competence, while negative feedback undermines it.[3] In addition, it appears that people are much more sensitive to negative feedback than to positive feedback. So, if one of your purposes is to amplify the sense of competence of your team members, you will want to focus on the positive that is being accomplished through their efforts. This has been called an "appreciative" stance.[4] Again, you are not ignoring the room for continued improvement. You can help and encourage team members to keep improving their performance as you also recognize the competence and improvement that have been occurring. If you continually focus on the deficiencies that remain, in contrast, you will be consistently undermining your team members' sense of competence. Your comments will basically be experienced as punishing.

Recognizing Skill

This innate need for appreciation is not a selfish, superficial craving for the center spotlight; it is an authentic, deep-seated desire to be deemed as worthy when offering something of worth.

TERRENCE DEAL AND M.K. KEY[5]

When you give team members recognition for the competence of their work, you are doing a number of important things. For example, you are strengthening the message that good work is important, valued, and noticed. You are appreciating the effort and accomplishment involved—providing a kind of "thank you" for a team member's contribution on behalf of the team and the organization. But perhaps most important, you are also validating and amplifying that team member's sense of competence. For a moment, the two of you step back from task activity, view the work in perspective, and together appreciate how well it was done.

It is important for you to be aware of any biases you may have that prevent you from appreciating the competence of your team members. Favoritism will breed cynicism and resentment, of course. However, another kind of bias is also worth looking out for. Walt Tymon and I found in our research that some individuals are generally less likely to recognize competence than others. These people are quick to attribute good performance to other factors—an easy task, other people's help, or luck. Low scores on our measure of "skill recognition" were related to lower feelings of competence.[6] Look out for that tendency—it damages intrinsic motivation. You want to be generous in recognizing the competence of your team members.

Managing Challenge

What I have called flow experiences. . . . Athletes refer to it as being in the zone. . . . Flow tends to occur when a person's skills are fully involved in overcoming a challenge that is just about manageable.

MIHALY CSIKSZENTMIHALYI[7]

People perform best when there is a fit between their ability and the task difficulty, or challenge. If the task is too easy, their attention wanders and they become bored. If it's too difficult, they get anxious and do less than their best work. An ideally challenging task is just manageable and requires full concentration. Because the task is challenging, it inspires even more satisfaction when it is performed well. The psychologist Mihaly Csikszentmihalyi, whose name is itself a challenge, has written a number of books on the fit between skill and challenge.[8] He reports that people are most likely to be fully engaged in their work activities when skills and challenges are both high and matched. He refers to this experience of full engagement as a sense of "flow"—what others have called being "in the zone."

As leader, then, you'll want to try to keep your team members close to this condition of optimal challenge. One way you can do this is through work assignments, making sure that skills are adequate to the difficulties, but that the difficulties are challenging. For workers who have held and mastered the same job for lengthy periods, consider assigning extra duties that require learning new skills, such as special projects or the mentoring of younger team members. Another way to create challenge is by helping to set even higher, more challenging standards as the team gets more skilled at its work.

Fostering High, Noncomparative Standards

No one can enjoy his work if he will be ranked with others.

W. EDWARDS DEMING[9]

In the self-management of the new work, standards of competence have to be internalized by workers. Standards have to matter to workers—to be important to them—if workers are to strive for standards and feel rewarded by meeting them. This caring about competence, of course, won't be independent of the other issues they care about. So, as leader, it will be useful to think about helping to create a culture of competence in a team. This means making sure that team members see the connection between competence standards and the other core issues that the team cares about—specifically its vision, its values, and its understanding of customer needs.

As you talk with your team members about these standards, you'll probably find that some of the standards your team cares about will tap into core values that attracted people to this career and organization to begin with. Consider the differences between the Marine Corps, the nursing profession, engineering, and the arts. Each embodies different virtues or types of standards and attracts people who value those virtues—courage and loyalty, compassion, precision, and creativity, respectively. What virtues or work values are most important to your team members? If you're not sure, you'd better talk with them about it.

Some performance standards may be obvious and will serve to provide minimum competence standards. Encouraging higher standards is an important part of building a culture of competence, but it is often impossible to spell out those standards in detail because of the uncertainties involved in the new work. For this reason, many leaders use lots of stories about competent acts to give workers concrete examples. Such stories get retold to new workers and become part of the team's culture. For example, James Collins and Jerry Pores, in *Built to Last*, explained how Nordstrom gives its employees the single standard of "outstanding customer service" and tells them to use their good judgment to achieve it. But new "Nordies," they add, are also told story after story to help make this standard real—stories about cheerfully gift wrapping items purchased from other stores, for example, and about ironing a shirt for a customer who needs it that afternoon.[10]

As you work at fostering high standards, it is important that you embody those standards yourself. Again, this type of consistency helps build your credibility. This leadership by example also provides a visible model for team members—a role model for others to copy. Team members may begin adding stories about your performance to the team's culture. If you hold yourself to a lower standard—for whatever reason—your statements on competence will seem hypocritical and are likely to be disregarded. You will lose your moral authority to set standards.

Finally, it is important not to let the personnel system drive your team members' sense of competence. W. Edwards Deming pointed out the dangers of employee performance systems that force ranked comparisons of workers or enforce a grading curve—so that the competence of the average worker gets mathematically set at "mediocre." Your goal, after all, is not to have a team that sees its work as mediocre or average. Rather, the ideal would be to have a team of high performers who feel proud of their work but who also understand that promotion slots and merit raises are limited. While I was on the faculty of the Graduate School of Business at the University of Pittsburgh, I was fortunate to have a dean, Gerald Zoffer, who was skilled at that balance of recognition and practical understanding. I received a number of appreciative letters and notes from him, which helped my sense of competence. Then when the time for merit pay increases arrived, we would all receive letters that began by apologizing for the limited pool of available funds, which he emphasized was less than we deserved given the high quality of work by our faculty. That approach worked well for my intrinsic motivation. By contrast, I know of other leaders who feel obliged to begin criticizing work competence early in the performance cycle so that workers will accept the modest pay raise as justified. What a motivational waste!

■ ■ ■

Next, we will look at building your team's sense of *progress*.

Reflections

1. Can you think of any ways to help team members get knowledge that would build helpful competencies—for example, through mentoring, courses, or meetings with experts within your organization?

2. Is there anything that makes it difficult for you to give appreciative feedback to the members of your team? If so, what can you do about it?

3. Is it a natural act for you to give team members credit for their successes, rather than saying they were lucky, the task was easy, or giving other explanations? If it's not a natural act, how can you begin doing it anyway?

4. Are there members of your team who do not face a level of challenge that requires their full engagement? If so, how might you provide a more optimal level of challenge for them?

5. Do you have a culture of competence in the team, with high performance standards that tap into team members' underlying values? If not, how could you help to build it?

17

Leading for Progress

This chapter will guide you in building a sense of progress in your team. The sense of progress comes from the final step in self-management—ensuring that the team is actually accomplishing its purpose.

As a leader, you can contribute to your team members' experience of progress in a number of ways. You can help build a climate that supports progress, make sure that team members get a rich supply of evidence to measure progress, and take time to recognize and celebrate their progress.

There are thus five building blocks of progress:

- Collaborative climate
- Milestones
- Celebrations
- Access to customers
- Measurement of improvement

Building a Collaborative Climate

Come let us reason together.

ANONYMOUS

Over the years, I've done a lot of research on conflict. Perhaps you've already used the *Thomas-Kilmann Conflict Mode Instrument* that Ralph Kilmann and I developed. I'm mentioning that material again here because the amount of progress your team members make will depend heavily on how they deal with the inevitable conflicts that come up within the team. If they butt heads and compete with each other, for example, they will become obstacles to each other and slow each other down. As a leader, you will want to help build a collaborative climate in the team, where team members support each other's progress on important tasks.

Figure 16 shows a model of five "conflict-handling modes."[1] Conflict occurs when the concerns of two people appear to be incompatible—to interfere with each other in some way. When people attempt to deal with the conflict, then, their behavior can be described along two basic dimensions. They are assertive to the extent that they try to satisfy their own concerns. They are cooperative to the extent that they try to meet the other person's concerns. Note that these dimensions are independent: they are *not* opposites. As the figure shows, collaborating is both assertive and cooperative. It involves trying to find an "integrative" (or win-win) solution that completely satisfies both their own concern and the other person's concern—that allows them both to make progress on their tasks.

Some people are skeptical about the possibility of integrative solutions, so here is a familiar example from international relations. In September 1978, the Camp David Accords settled a competitive

Figure 16. **Five Conflict-Handling Modes**

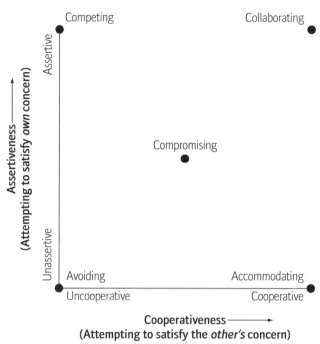

dispute between Israel and Egypt over the West Bank region that Israel had taken in an earlier war. The breakthrough occurred at Camp David when President Jimmy Carter helped steer negotiations in a more collaborative direction. He helped each side identify its primary underlying concern—the issue it cared most strongly about. For Egypt, it was regaining sovereignty over its historic land; for Israel, it was the security of having a safe geographic area along its border. Realizing this, and gradually accepting the legitimacy of each other's concerns, they tried with President Carter's help to find a way of satisfying both concerns. The result was the return of the land to Egypt and the creation of a neutral United Nations force to maintain safety in that territory—an integrative outcome that advanced both sets of purposes.[2]

Consider what a *collaborative* climate means in a work setting. People listen to their team members' concerns, take them seriously, and try to facilitate them—as well as their own. Energy is directed into problem solving to advance all the tasks. To be sure, team members aren't always able to find integrative solutions; sometimes they have to settle for compromise. But they tend to make more overall progress than groups that never try. As a leader, isn't that the way you want your team to operate?

For contrast, consider the other conflict-handling modes and their effects on progress. *Avoiding* (unassertive and uncooperative) is a lose-lose mode: you don't address the conflict, so you wind up neglecting both your own and the other person's concerns. When avoiding is prominent, tasks commonly get put on hold and little progress occurs. Competing, compromising, and accommodating are win-lose modes: you assume that both people can't win, so you focus on deciding who wins and who loses. *Competing* (assertive and uncooperative) happens when you try to satisfy your own concerns at the other person's expense. When competing is typical, energy gets directed against other team members, and many deadlocks block progress. *Accommodating* (unassertive and cooperative) happens when you sacrifice your own concerns to satisfy the other person. When accommodating is the norm, people act cooperatively during meetings, but are usually left frustrated, which often leads to hallway complaining after the meeting and a lack of cooperation in actually implementing decisions. Finally, *compromising* (intermediate in assertiveness and cooperativeness) occurs when you settle for half a loaf—half of what each of you really wants. This mode results in expedient, partial sacrifices of both task concerns, leaving everyone with some progress, but less than they want.

For resources on building collaboration, see the notes for this chapter.[3]

Tracking Milestones

All motion is relative.

PRINCIPLE OF PHYSICS

Consider what this principle means. You and I are whizzing through space at an incredible speed as we circle the sun, as the sun moves in its spiral galaxy, and as the universe keeps expanding. Yet this movement doesn't register for us because we are not passing fixed, visible reference points. We need reference points to measure movement and progress. Chapter 14 discussed the importance of providing a detailed picture of a vision so as to make work meaningful. The point then was that these details would make the vision more real or compelling. Here, the point is that these same details provide the milestones that help you recognize that the purpose is actually being accomplished.

Milestones are especially important on longer tasks. Consider for a moment the difference between the work activities you perform and the purpose you're pursuing. On a day-to-day basis, you do work activities, and you watch for progress toward the purpose. On longer tasks, that progress is very gradual. You may literally need to complete thousands of steps before you finish your part of the work. You know intellectually that each step advances the work, but there are so many steps to take that each step seems to make an imperceptible difference. It's a lot like taking a long hike. At the worst moments, the work can seem to go on forever, and you seem to be trudging. What you need, then, are milestones that mark recognizable progress and help keep you energized.

Milestones break up a task into psychologically significant advances. Think for a moment about why books like this one are divided into chapters. Clearly, one reason is to help you experience a sense of progress as you read through it—to reinforce your continued reading. I can also tell you that it is helping me, as the writer, feel a sense of progress as I write. As a leader, then, it is important to make sure that your team members have clear milestones—without lengthy gaps between them—to mark their progress on longer tasks.

As you help your team track milestones, keep in mind that some milestones toward the purpose occur after your team's portion of the work is completed. For example, I find that I am still energized by news of the ongoing citations of some articles and the sales of training instruments that I wrote over twenty years ago! Likewise, new proposals made by your team may be adopted and implemented by top management, or new products they have designed may be produced or sold. These downstream milestones are often the most important parts of achieving the purpose so it will be useful to continue tracking this progress and reporting it to the team.

Celebrating Progress

Without rite and ceremony. . . . Life becomes an endless set of Wednesdays.

LEE BOLMAN AND TERRENCE DEAL, CITING D. CAMPBELL[4]

Some people are uneasy thinking about celebrations of progress. This seems to be one of those areas where our metaphors sometimes get in the way. People often talk about tasks as though they were short races—sprints. In a sprint, it is truly risky to celebrate your progress during the event. In the famous words of Satchel Paige, "Don't look back. Something may be gaining on you."[5]

The trouble is that most significant tasks in the new-work world are not sprints. They may include a few stages that are like sprints, where there is intense time pressure to meet a requirement. But, overall, they stretch over a longer time frame and give team members time to plan and make choices—not just to perform activities as swiftly as possible. On these kinds of tasks, then, people need to track their progress so as to make intelligent choices. Equally important, they need to celebrate their progress in some way to keep themselves energized.

A celebration is a time to pause, recognize that a significant milestone has been reached, and savor that fact. Recall that intrinsic motivation is about the energy produced by positive emotions about work. Celebrations can be private, of course, but sharing them seems to amplify or intensify those emotions.

As a leader, then, you can create a climate that encourages task celebrations, as well as starting some of those celebrations yourself. Sometimes it will be enough to simply pause during a meeting and note that an event is another sign of progress for the team. You may also want to briefly review the entire task to date, to show how far the team has come. I find that these simple "appreciative pauses" with colleagues have become very important during my own projects. Of course, some celebrations deserve to be more elaborate, depending on the significance of the event, the work schedule, and your organization's culture. Terrence Deal and M. K. Key provide some creative examples of celebrations in their book, *Corporate Celebration*.[6]

Providing Access to Customers

The entire organization has to be structured so that employees can get feedback from customers about their performance and their responses to customer needs.

EDWARD LAWLER[7]

At a dinner show several years ago, I found myself seated next to a respected consultant who specialized in job design. When I mentioned that I was studying intrinsic motivation, he said something with such conviction that it has stayed with me: "The most important thing is to let workers work with customers." Ed Lawler, likewise, writes about giving workers a direct "line of sight" to the customer.[8]

The quality movement emphatically reminded us that meeting the needs of customers, whether internal or external, is the main justification for work tasks. Earlier in the book, I discussed how the notion of helping customers is often what makes a work purpose meaningful. For that reason, customer satisfaction and appreciation is often the most direct evidence of ongoing accomplishment.

There are a number of ways of getting evidence of customer satisfaction, of course. Sales figures, customer surveys, and letters of appreciation are important indicators of customer satisfaction. But for emotional impact, they are a poor substitute for direct, face-to-face encounters. There you can see the smile, feel the handshake, and hear the depth of feeling behind what the customer says. That's one of the reasons why politicians like to meet with constituents and "press the flesh." They aren't just winning votes; they're also reenergizing themselves. Likewise, actors and entertainers commonly speak of the energy they get from a live audience, as opposed to simply taping or filming a performance for the camera.

As a leader, then, you'll want to do what you can to provide workers with direct access to customers. Many jobs already have customer contact built in, of course. Researchers like Hackman and Oldham have shown that it is possible to build customer contact into a variety of other jobs.[9] For example, clerical workers who process insurance files can be given responsibility for contacting customers directly to resolve problems. At a minimum, you can find ways of creating occasional meetings between your team members and some of the customers affected by their work.

Measuring Improvements (and Reducing Cycle Time)

Post measurements of progress conspicuously. Simple, visible measures of what's important. . . .

TOM PETERS[10]

Recurring tasks are made up of cycles of activities. Another lesson from the quality movement is that measuring the outcomes of these cycles (how well the purpose is being achieved) gives workers the feedback needed to improve that cycle. In terms of the self-management model in chapter 3, measuring whether outcomes are improving allows you to test the effectiveness of your choices and to track the effects of work competence. Measuring the rate of improvement is also important to workers' feelings of progress.

The challenge here is to measure the right results. From a motivational point of view, you need to measure the outcomes that you and your team care about—those aspects of the task purpose that flow from your team's vision. These measures show the value-added of your efforts in achieving that vision. Don't just settle for what's easy to measure. If you run training programs, for example, it is unlikely that your team members will get excited about simply offering more programs per year. What are you trying to accomplish with this training? How could you measure that convincingly? And, as the quote from Tom Peters suggests, why not post the results prominently?

In any measurement program, *cycle time* is one of the most useful operational elements to track—and work to reduce. Ultimately, reducing cycle time is not about people running harder to cover the distance faster. It has more to do with redesigning and simplifying processes so that your team members have to cover fewer steps and climb over fewer obstacles. As noted earlier, eliminating steps that add little value to the task purpose makes work more meaningful, and eliminating unnecessary approvals increases workers' sense of choice. The point here is that these same improvements increase team members' sense of *speed*—helping them move from "trudging" to "cooking."

As a leader, then, you will want to measure cycle time for key tasks and then to keep looking for ways of simplifying the processes involved—while enlisting team members' help. There are a number of tools for simplifying work processes, from suggestion boxes to process charting and reengineering.

Reflections

1. How collaborative is the climate within your work team? Are some people less collaborative than others? What can you do to help them change their behavior?

2. On longer work tasks or projects, are there clear milestones that will help the team recognize the progress it is making? If not, how can you help provide them?

3. Is there anything that makes you reluctant to celebrate the progress that your team members are making? How can you overcome that reluctance?

4. Do the members of your team have direct contact with their internal or external customers—the people who benefit most from their work? If not, how can you provide that sort of contact—or other compelling evidence that their work is benefiting and/or delighting the people they are trying to help?

5. Are you measuring the most important results of your team's work, so that the team can recognize the progress it cares most about? Can you think of ways of reducing the cycle time on recurrent tasks—by eliminating unnecessary steps that contribute little value and slow things down?

18

Enjoying the Ride

We'll begin this final chapter with a review of key ideas and then end with a final bit of advice.

Summary

The key ideas in this book are summarized below.

Work Has Changed Dramatically

Research shows that a sea change has occurred in the nature of work within the space of a single generation. People used to think of work in terms of the activities (behaviors) that workers needed to perform. Bureaucratic organizations used close supervision and elaborate rules to make sure workers performed those activities properly, and the job of workers was mostly to comply with this sort of command-and-control management. By the 1990s, however, the environment had begun to change too rapidly for bureaucratic rules and close supervision to handle. Those uncertainties overwhelmed bureaucratic organizations and forced a flattening of the hierarchy and drastic reductions in organizational rules. When this happened, work changed in fundamental ways. Workers have had to take responsibility for handling much of the uncertainty surrounding their jobs. They are required to be more proactive and to make many of the decisions formerly made by managers.

The Essence of Today's Work Is Self-Management

Today's work is not simply about performing activities; it is now about workers' directing their own activities toward organizational purposes. The worker's role, then, has shifted from passive compliance to proactive self-management. Self-management involves a series of four steps by which today's workers direct their work toward the accomplishment of organizational purposes:

- Committing to a *meaningful* work purpose
- *Choosing* activities that will best accomplish the purpose
- Checking to make sure they are performing those activities *competently*
- Checking to make sure that they are actually making *progress* toward accomplishing the purpose

Self-Management Requires a Different Kind of Motivation—Intrinsic Motivation

Self-management requires a deeper level of commitment than the old compliance-era work, since workers must now be committed to the purpose they are pursuing. The new work is also more psychologically demanding, involving a great deal more judgment and decision making. Although money and other extrinsic rewards remain important to workers, it is clear that the new work requires much more than that. Effective self-management depends heavily on intrinsic rewards—the psychological rewards that workers can get from self-management itself. There are four key intrinsic rewards:

- Sense of meaningfulness—the feeling that one is pursuing a worthy work purpose, one that is worth one's time and energy
- Sense of choice—the sense that one is able to make one's own decisions and act out of one's own understanding of the work
- Sense of competence—the feeling that one is performing work activities well, that one is doing high-quality work
- Sense of progress—the sense that one is actually achieving the work purpose

Employee Engagement Is Energized by Intrinsic Rewards

Today's organizations have had to coin a new phrase, "employee engagement," to address the unique motivational needs of today's workers. However, the term has been used loosely to mean many different things. Employee engagement is defined here as active self-management—the key requirement of today's work. In turn, employee engagement is powered and sustained by the intrinsic rewards generated by self-management itself—by the sense of meaningfulness, the sense of choice, the sense of competence, and the sense of progress that come from effective self-management. Research findings show the powerful effects of the intrinsic rewards—on performance, professional development, job satisfaction, retention, organizational loyalty, and reduced stress. These four intrinsic rewards, then, are the psychological vital signs of an engaged work force. They provide a relatively healthy, positive, and sustainable form of motivation.

Leaders Need a Diagnostic Framework to Build Engagement

Organizations and their leaders have been trying many different tactics, in a hit-or-miss way, to try to enhance engagement. Likewise, career-counseling books have promoted different strategies to help job holders make their work more rewarding. This book provides a two-step set of diagnostics to give you a more efficient way of diagnosing engagement problems and providing the conditions needed to enhance engagement. The first step involves determining the levels of the four key intrinsic rewards to see whether low engagement is due to a deficiency in meaningfulness, choice, competence, or progress—because their sources and remedies are quite different. The second step involves examining the key building blocks for each intrinsic reward, as a kind of checklist to see which building blocks for that reward may be missing. This decision tree leads to a set of actions to help create the missing building block.

It Is Important for Leaders to Learn to Manage Their Own Intrinsic Rewards

Workshops have shown that it is much easier for leaders to lead for engagement when they first learn how to manage their own intrinsic rewards. Developing this skill helps you recognize the intrinsic rewards in your employees, gives you more credibility, and—as a bonus—helps you stay more engaged and energized. So this book has provided rich descriptions of the experience of being high or low in each reward, to help you recognize and chart your own levels of the rewards. We have then discussed sets of actions that you can take to help create the building blocks that boost each reward in your own job.

Leading for Engagement Is a Matter of Following Basic Principles

Engaging employees is not a matter of personality or charisma. This book has provided a number of general guidelines or tips that include focusing on the steps of self-management, playing a positive role, listening and enabling, providing credible evidence for the intrinsic rewards, explaining your leadership philosophy, de-emphasizing money as a motivator, and working to engage the "motivational middle." It has also provided observable signs of the four intrinsic rewards in groups to help you chart their current levels in your team and to set some priorities for deciding which intrinsic rewards need the most attention. We then discussed sets of leadership actions that you can take to create the building blocks for any of the intrinsic rewards that require your attention.

So now you're ready to get started.

A Final Word

In this book, I have provided as much information and bits of coaching as I could on how you can lead for engagement. But it would be pretty ironic if you interpreted it as just another set of activities you had to comply with. So it's worth emphasizing that leading for engagement is an important purpose in today's workplace and that to be effective at it (and to enjoy it), you'll want to do it in a self-managing way. So remember the following guidelines as you begin:

- You are committing to a meaningful purpose—one that will engage your team members, energize them, tap into their intelligence and creativity, and achieve the kinds of milestones and development you and they will be proud of. Formulate a vision that "sings" for you and your team.

- You will want to use your intelligence and creativity to choose the best ways of doing this in your unit. Treat the recommendations in this book as guidelines and suggestions only. Once you understand the basic ideas, feel free to experiment and try new ideas. Drive your own engagement train and have fun with it. If you come up with something creative that you are especially proud of, send me an e-mail and let me know about it.

- Enjoy the fact that you will probably be developing some new competencies as you begin to lead for engagement. And give yourself a break as you work your way up the learning curve. You may feel a little awkward at first, but focus on the improvements and the learning. Give yourself credit for your successes. I find it helps to think of leading for engagement as an adventure.

- Watch for, and savor, the little (or big) signs of progress in your team's self-management—signs of commitment and enthusiasm, bits of initiative and creativity, a sense of momentum, greater collaboration, and performance breakthroughs.

Again, enjoy the adventure! And if you find that this book works for you, please share it with your boss and others in your organization. Help to create a culture of engagement that will keep everyone energized and productive!

Two Earlier Models of Intrinsic Motivation

Why did my colleagues and I need to develop a new list of intrinsic rewards—didn't we already have models of intrinsic motivation? Yes, there were a couple of popular models dating from the 1960s. However, both of these older models left out important intrinsic rewards that are central to the self-management process. I'll briefly describe them here so that you can see how the new model builds on them.[1]

The most widely known model of intrinsic motivation was originally developed by Edward Deci, a psychologist at the University of Rochester.[2] Much of his later academic work on the model has been with Richard Ryan.[3] Deci also wrote a popular book with Richard Flaste, *Why We Do What We Do*, which summarized his views.[4] His model is based largely on a rigorous program of laboratory research involving experimental games such as anagrams (word scrambles). It is especially well known in the field of education. For my purposes, its main shortcoming is that the model focuses only on task activities as sources of intrinsic rewards, so that purposes are excluded. In Deci's model, task activities are intrinsically rewarding when people experience a sense of self-determination (choice) and of competence. The model I've presented in this book builds on Deci's model by adding the rewards that come from task purposes, namely meaningfulness and progress. This is a key improvement in applying the model to work tasks involving more serious purposes. Deci also made the controversial assertion that extrinsic rewards tend to reduce intrinsic rewards. Recent research reviews have found very little support for this effect, especially in organizational settings.[5] The model I describe in this book sees no inherent conflict between intrinsic and extrinsic rewards. (For more on this idea, see resource B.)

The second model of intrinsic motivation was developed by Richard Hackman, now at Harvard University, and Greg Oldham of the University of Illinois.[6] It has been used widely in organizational settings, where it has largely replaced Frederick Herzberg's theory of motivators and hygiene factors.[7] The Hackman and Oldham model is often called the "job characteristics" model because it describes the effects of five dimensions of job design: skill variety, task identity, task significance, autonomy, and feedback. Research shows that these job dimensions generally have an impact on job satisfaction and other outcomes. However, there is less support for the motivational core of the model.[8] That part of the model says that intrinsic motivation occurs when three "psychological states" are present: experienced *meaningfulness* of the work, experienced *responsibility for outcomes* of the work, and *knowledge of actual results* of the work. For my purposes, this list had two shortcomings. First, it focuses only on task outcomes (similar to purposes) as a factor in intrinsic motivation, leaving out activity-related rewards. Second, only meaningfulness is clearly an intrinsic reward, as in the current model. My current model, then, collapsed Hackman and Oldham's three psychological states into two intrinsically rewarding states—a sense of meaningfulness and of progress—and then added the missing activity-related rewards—a sense of choice and of competence.

Putting Money in Perspective

This material is my attempt to help you think clearly about the role of money in this era of self-management and intrinsic motivation.

People who study work motivation find it helpful to separate two kinds of behaviors—*membership* behavior (joining an organization and remaining) and *performance* behavior (how one does the work). Let's start with membership behavior.

Taking a Job and Remaining

Consider the role of money in people's lives. For most of us, money isn't an end in itself; it's a means to satisfy other ends. Some exceptions exist of course—people who measure their worth and success almost solely in terms of money. But for the vast majority of us, money is simply something that gives us choices for taking care of areas of our lives that are important—including family and friends, our health, and rewarding work. We try to manage our finances with the goal of managing them well enough so that we have to make few sacrifices in those areas we value. Most of us don't try to maximize our money in isolation from our other needs because we learn that this kind of single-mindedness can sacrifice our relationships with family and friends and our health or lead us to take on work that is unfulfilling.

The importance of money in taking a job depends partly on the amount of financial cushion or slack you have—the difference between what you have and your basic needs. That cushion gives you choices. With a large cushion, you can afford not to take the highest-paying jobs. You can take government service jobs or other lower-paying jobs with high intrinsic rewards, try self-employment, or even primarily do volunteer work. With no cushion, on the other hand, you may have to take the first job that comes along or to choose among jobs based on money alone. For most of us in between, with some cushion, money is a significant consideration in taking a job. We want pay and benefits to be in the range for comparable jobs—that is, to be fair. And more pay is better than less. But modest differences in pay are outweighed by differences in the intrinsic rewards that the jobs offer.

My experience, then, is that intrinsic rewards play a strong role in shaping most people's careers. People pick careers they believe will be intrinsically rewarding and choose to stay on a job or not based largely on the intrinsic rewards they actually receive. When those rewards decline, they get unhappy and start looking for other, more rewarding jobs. Large increases in pay (in new "career opportunities") can also direct them to new jobs within their career of choice, and unfair pay can cause them to begin looking for other jobs. But it is the intrinsic rewards that flow from the day-to-day work that tend to keep most of us coming back to a job.

Performing Well

What makes workers perform well? It depends on what you mean by "performing well." If you only mean following directions—that is, compliance—then extrinsic rewards will fill the bill. Make a sizable part of pay dependent upon compliance, find a way of verifying compliance, and that should do it. But you'll have to live with the familiar pathologies of extrinsic reward systems—your workers will be doing their jobs only well enough to get by, neglecting what is not measured, and finding ways of gaming the system.

On the .other hand, if performing well means self-management, then you'll need intrinsic motivation. This sort of motivation involves commitment to the task itself. It comes from doing what one honestly believes is best for promoting the task purpose and work quality. It motivates workers to deal with uncertainties in the new work that can't be anticipated by the people who design pay systems. It also motivates workers to do their best even when nobody is looking.

As I was finishing the first edition of this book, a study was published that is relevant here.[1] That study measured the combined effects of pay-for-performance compensation systems and employees' commitment to their organizations' values. Without commitment to their organizations' values, pay-for-performance made employees *less likely* to do tasks that would help the organizations' purposes but weren't measured as part of their duties. When employees were committed to the organizations' values, however, pay-for-performance didn't discourage that extra effort. People performed above and beyond the call of duty because they cared, even if it wasn't extrinsically rewarded.

If you've agreed with the thinking of this book, then, you'll want to help build intrinsic motivation in work teams. This means making sure that as many as possible of the building blocks are there for creating a sense of *meaningfulness, choice, competence,* and *progress* in workers' jobs.

But pay is still important to most workers. This raises the question of how to treat it.

Treating Pay as an Equity Issue

On performance issues, I think of extrinsic motivation as something that supplements intrinsic motivation. In other words, extrinsic incentives can have a greater influence on behavior when intrinsic motivation is moderate to low. But if intrinsic motivation is already high—with people self-managing and highly energized—monetary incentives provide little or no additional force. Past some point, it simply becomes impossible to be more motivated in any sustainable way. So if you are successful in building high intrinsic motivation, don't expect your pay system to have a major positive effect on performance.

With pay systems, on the whole, the best you can hope for is perceived fairness—or equity—so that pay doesn't become a distractor. *Equity* is a principle of fairness that basically says that your outcomes (rewards) should be proportional to your inputs (performance). It comes into play in comparisons between people or groups and only becomes a motivational force when it is violated. Equity is violated when workers see that others in comparable jobs are paid more for the same level of performance or when they find that others are paid the same even though they are performing at lower levels. When that happens, pay issues take center stage for workers, and people want to remedy the situation. But when pay is seen as equitable, workers' attention can return to their work tasks.

What does it mean to treat pay as primarily an equity issue? It means making sure that pay reflects performance in a reasonable manner, so that workers see that they are treated fairly. It means trying to avoid perceived inequities and to fix those that do occur. It does not mean assuming that workers are doing good work primarily to get higher pay. Wanting fair "pay for performance" is not the same as "performing for the pay."

When you talk with workers about motivational issues, put the *task* in the foreground—where it belongs—and put pay in the background. Talk about the intrinsic rewards and the building blocks. Stressing pay incentives is likely to insult workers who are committed to the task purpose and will introduce an element of cynicism into the climate. As a practical matter, a pay-for-performance system will still provide backup extrinsic motivation for a worker who is not highly intrinsically motivated. But the last thing you want to do is to assume that your workers are motivated extrinsically and to treat them in that way.

NOTES

Chapter 1

1. James O'Toole and Edward E. Lawler III, *The New American Workplace* (New York: Palgrave Macmillan, 2006). This book was commissioned by the Society for Human Resource Management as a follow-up to a landmark 1973 book on the state of the American workplace, *Work in America*, which had been commissioned by the U.S. Secretary of Health, Education, and Welfare.
2. See Richard E. Walton, "From Control to Commitment in the Workplace," *Harvard Business Review* 63, no. 2 (1985): 77–84.
3. Warren G. Bennis, "The Coming Death of Bureaucracy," *Think Magazine*, November–December 1966, 30–35. For an update on this theme, see Gifford Pinchot and Elizabeth Pinchot, *The End of Bureaucracy and the Rise of the Intelligent Organization* (San Francisco: Berrett-Koehler, 1994).
4. O'Toole and Lawler. *The New American Workplace*, 5.
5. Jeffrey Pfeffer, *Competitive Advantage Through People: Unleashing the Power of the Work Force* (Boston: Harvard Business School Press, 1992).
6. Quoted in Noel M. Tichy and Stratford Sherman, *Control Your Destiny or Someone Else Will: How Jack Welch Is Making General Electric the World's Most Competitive Corporation* (New York: Currency Doubleday, 1993), 251.
7. O'Toole and Lawler, *The New American Workplace*, 47, report that the percentage of Fortune 1000 firms reporting job enrichment efforts had risen to 86 percent by 2005. Likewise, the percentage using self-managing teams had risen to 65 percent.
8. See William H. Macey and Benjamin Schneider, "The Meaning of Employee Engagement," *Industrial and Organizational Psychology* 1, no. 1 (March 2008), 3–30.

Chapter 2

1. Kenneth W. Thomas and Betty A. Velthouse, "Cognitive Elements of Empowerment: An Interpretive Model of Intrinsic Task Motivation," *Academy of Management Review* 15, no. 14 (1990): 666–681.

2. I have found Jay Galbraith's thinking most helpful in understanding how and why organizations have needed to change structure to cope with increased uncertainties in their environment. My analysis draws heavily upon his concepts. His ideas were developed in Jay Galbraith, *Designing Complex Organizations* (Reading, MA: Addison-Wesley, 1973) and in a number of subsequent books and are heavily cited in most management texts.

3. The notion of uncertainty absorption was developed in James G. March and Herbert A. Simon, *Organizations* (New York: Wiley, 1958). The idea of buffering the organization's technical core from environmental influences was described in James D. Thompson, *Organizations in Action* (New York: McGraw-Hill, 1967). Both works were seminal in the development of the organizational sciences.

4. Peter Block, *Stewardship: Choosing Service Over Self-Interest* (San Francisco: Berrett-Koehler, 1993).

5. Frederick W. Taylor, *The Principles of Scientific Management* (New York: Harper & Row, 1911).

6. The breakthrough book on the effect of technology on organization was Joan Woodward, *Industrial Organization: Theory and Practice* (London: Oxford University Press, 1965). Breakthrough books on the effects of environmental uncertainty were Tom Burns and George M. Stalker, *The Management of Innovation* (London: Tavistock, 1961), and Paul R. Lawrence and Jay W. Lorsch, *Organization and Environment* (Homewood, IL: Irwin, 1969).

7. Peter B. Vaill, *Managing as a Performing Art* (San Francisco: Jossey-Bass, 1989), 2–3.

8. Statistics cited in O'Toole and Lawler, *The New American Workplace*.

9. Richard J. Leider, *The Power of Purpose* (San Francisco: Berrett-Koehler, 2004), 137.

10. Joseph Campbell, *The Hero with a Thousand Faces* (Princeton, NJ: Princeton University Press, 1989).

11. The Viennese psychiatrist Victor Frankl, who himself survived the Nazi death camps, wrote powerfully of the importance of purpose in sustaining life, founding an influential branch of psychiatry based on that principle. The story of his experience, which also contained his philosophy, was an international best seller in the 1950s and 1960s: Victor E. Frankl, *Man's Search for Meaning: An Introduction to Logotherapy* (New York: Washington Square Press, 1963).

12. Albert Camus, *The Myth of Sisyphus and Other Essays* (New York: Random House, 1955).

13. Studs Terkel, *Working* (New York: Ballantine, 1985), xiii.

14. For a description of the changing workforce and its implications for organizations, see David Jamieson and Julie O'Mara, *Managing Workforce 2000* (San Francisco: Jossey-Bass, 1991).

15. These generational differences have been analyzed in a number of books. See, for example, Robert Wendover, *Crossing the Generational Divide—From Boomers to Zoomers* (Shawnee Mission, KS: National Press Publications, 2007).

16. The distinction between transactional and transformational leadership was developed in the management literature by Bernard M. Bass, *Leadership and Performance Beyond Expectations* (New York: Free Press, 1985), using concepts from James McGregor Burns.

17. James M. Burns, *Leadership* (New York: Harper & Row, 1978).

18. For example: Bass, *Leadership and Performance Beyond Expectations*; Warren Bennis and Burt Nanus, *Leaders: The Strategies for Taking Charge* (New York: Harper & Row, 1985); James Kouzes and Barry Posner, *The Leadership Challenge* (San Francisco: Jossey-Bass, 1987).

19. James C. Collins and Jerry I. Porras, *Built to Last: Successful Habits of Visionary Companies* (New York: HarperCollins, 2002).

20. Collins and Porras, *Built to Last*; A. De Geus, "Companies: What Are They?" *RSA Journal*, June 1995, 26–35.

21. De Geus, "Companies: What Are They?" 29, cited in Lee G. Bolman and Terrence E. Deal, *Reframing Organizations*, 4th ed. (San Francisco: Jossey-Bass, 2004), 399.

22. Block, *Stewardship*, 5.

23. See, for example, Robert S. Kaplan and David P. Norton, "Using the Balanced Scorecard as a Strategic Management System," *Harvard Business Review*, 85, nos. 7–8 (July–August 2007).

24. This philosophy is outlined in a short book by Bruce Vincent, *The 3rd Way: Accelerating Organizational Performance* (Golden, CO: New West Institute, 2005). This consulting firm has provided extensive field-testing of the material in this book and the *Work Engagement Profile*. New West provides consulting services for performance-based organizational change and transition coaching. Information about the New West Institute is available at http://www.newwestinstitute.com.

Chapter 3

1. A first version of this model appeared in a technical report prepared for the Eighth Quadrennial Review of Military Compensation: Kenneth W. Thomas and Erik Jansen, "Intrinsic Motivation in the Military: Models and Strategic Importance," (Technical Report NPS-SM-96-001, Monterey, CA: Naval Postgraduate School, September 1996). It was then adapted for broader publication in Kenneth W. Thomas, Erik Jansen, and Walter G. Tymon Jr., "Navigating in the Realm of Theory: An Empowering View of Construct Development," *Research in Organizational Change and Development* 10 (1997): 1–30.

2. Gordon R. Sullivan and Michael V. Harper, *Hope Is Not a Method: What Business Leaders Can Learn from America's Army* (New York: Random House, 1996).

3. For a discussion of the importance of initiative in today's work, see Michael Frese and Doris Fay, "Personal Initiative: An Active Performance Concept for Work in the 21st Century," in *Research in Organizational Behavior*, ed. B. M. Staw and R. I. Sutton, (New York: Elsevier, 2001), 23: 133–187.

4. John Dewey (1859–1952) was an influential American advocate of pragmatism in education and philosophy, stressing the fundamental role of intelligence and learning in solving the practical problems people encountered. See, for example, John Dewey, *How We Think* (Boston: Heath, 1933).

5. Peter M. Senge, *The Fifth Discipline: The Art and Practice of the Learning Organization* (New York: Doubleday, 1990).

6. John Gibbons, *Employee Engagement: A Review of Current Research and Its Implications*, Report E-0010-06-RR (New York: Conference Board, 2006); Vincent, *The 3rd Way*.

7. For a classic article on coaching, see Roger D. Evered and James C. Selman, "Coaching and the Art of Management," *Organization Dynamics* 18, no. 2 (Autumn 1989): 16–32.

8. Jack Welch's ideas have been publicized in a number of books. See Tichy and Sherman, *Control Your Destiny*. The idea of boundarylessness was elaborated on in a book by several of the main consultants to G.E.: Ron Ashkenas, Dave Ulrich, Todd Jick, and Steve Kerr, *The Boundaryless Organization: Breaking the Chains of Organizational Structure* (San Francisco: Jossey-Bass, 1995).

9. Block, *Stewardship*, 30.

10. Kenneth W. Thomas, Susan P. Hocevar, and Gail Fann Thomas, "Operational, Tactical, and Strategic Meanings of Empowerment: Historical Analysis, Interview Findings, and an Integrative Language" (Monterey, CA: Naval Postgraduate School, December 1998), 21.

Chapter 4

1. This set of intrinsic rewards has evolved over time as my colleagues and I have analyzed more data and refined our insights. Much of this evolution is described in Thomas, Jansen, and Tymon, "Navigating in the Realm of Theory." The first theoretical publication of the model, in Thomas and Velthouse, "Cognitive Elements of Empowerment," listed meaningfulness, choice, competence, and impact. In later empirical and theoretical work with Walt Tymon, it became clearer that what we had earlier referred to as "impact" in the model was actually a sense of progress.

2. See the extensive academic analysis of the concept of engagement in the article by Macey and Schneider, "The Meaning of Employee Engagement." Their conclusions about engagement as a psychological state emphasize positive emotions and are very consistent with the model in this book. They note, in fact, that there is very strong overlap between the concept of engagement and psychological "empowerment," which is the term we used in earlier versions of our research program.

3. Kenneth W. Thomas and Walter G. Tymon Jr., *Work Engagement Profile* (Mountain View, CA: CPP, 2009). (An earlier version of the *Work Engagement Profile* was originally published as the *Empowerment Inventory* by Xicom, in Tuxedo, NY, in 1993. Xicom was acquired in 1999 by CPP.)

4. Thomas and Tymon, *Work Engagement Profile*, 9.
5. This notion of life stages and transition has been familiar since the publication of two classic works in the 1970s. Daniel J. Levinson, *The Seasons of a Man's Life* (New York: Ballantine, 1979), and Gail Sheehy, *Passages: Predictable Crises of Adult Life* (New York: Dutton, 1976). See also the subsequent book by Daniel J. Levinson, *The Seasons of a Woman's Life* (New York: Ballantine, 1996).
6. For creative ways of enhancing this fit, see Jamieson and O'Mara, *Managing Workforce 2000*.
7. There have been a number of recent management books that mention soul or spirit in the context of finding meaning in work. Here are a few: Block, *Stewardship;* Leider, *The Power of Purpose;* Jack Hawley, *Reawakening the Spirit in Work* (San Francisco: Berrett-Koehler, 1993); Lee G. Bolman and Terrence E. Deal, *Leading with Soul* (San Francisco: Jossey-Bass, 1995); Keshavan Nair, *A Higher Standard of Leadership: Lessons from the Life of Gandhi* (San Francisco: Berrett-Koehler, 1994); and Alan Green, *A Company Discovers Its Soul* (San Francisco: Berrett-Koehler, 1996).
8. The three stages described here—dependence, counterdependence, and interdependence—are widely used now. They were introduced into the literature on organizational development by Warren G. Bennis and Herbert A. Shepard in "A Theory of Group Development," *Human Relations* 9, no. 4 (1956): 415–437.
9. Chris Argyris, *Personality and Organization: The Conflict Between System and the Individual* (New York: Harper & Brothers, 1957).
10. This is a frequent theme in the literature on codependency. See, for example, John Bradshaw, *Bradshaw on: The Family* (Deerfield Beach, FL: Health Communications, 1988).
11. For example, this definition of self was prominent in the est movement introduced by Werner Erhard in the 1970s. For a somewhat sympathetic biography and statement of the est philosophy, see William W. Bartley III, *Werner Erhard* (New York: Potter, 1978). More recently this same notion has been captured by viewing the self as "agent." See, for example, Barbara L. McCombs and R. J. Marzano, "Putting the Self in Self-Regulated Learning: The Self as Agent in Integrating Will and Skill," *Educational Psychologist* 31 (1990): 819–833.
12. Richard deCharms, *Personal Causation: The Internal Affective Determinants of Behavior* (New York: Academic Press, 1968).
13. This link between autonomy (choice) and experienced responsibility for outcomes was described in J. Richard Hackman and Greg R. Oldham, *Work Redesign* (Reading, MA: Addison-Wesley, 1980), 79, 80.
14. Robert W. White, "Motivation Reconsidered: The Concept of Competence," *Psychological Review* 66 (1959): 297–333.
15. Edward L. Deci, *Intrinsic Motivation* (New York: Plenum Press, 1975).
16. Dick Richards, *Artful Work: Awakening Joy, Meaning, and Commitment in the Workplace* (San Francisco: Berrett-Koehler, 1995).
17. Vaill, *Managing as a Performing Art*.

18. Mihaly Csikszentmihalyi, *Flow: The Psychology of Optimal Experience* (New York: Harper & Row, 1990).

19. Tom Peters, *Thriving on Chaos: Handbook for a Management Revolution* (New York: Harper Perennial, 1988), 366.

20. This quote is from a video, *Speed, Simplicity, and Self-Confidence: Jack Welch Talks with Warren Bennis* (Schaumburg, IL: Video Publishing House, 1993).

21. Thomas and Tymon, *Work Engagement Profile.*

22. Harry Levinson, "When Executives Burn Out," *Harvard Business Review* 59, no. 3 (May–June 1981): 72–81.

Chapter 5

1. This tendency was reported in an article by Chip Heath, "On the Social Psychology of Agency Relationships: Lay Theories of Motivation Overemphasize Extrinsic Incentives," *Organizational Behavior and Human Decision Processes* 78 (1999): 25–62.

2. Herbert A. Simon, "A Behavioral Model of Rational Choice," *Quarterly Journal of Economics* 69 (1955): 99–118.

3. Expectancy theory was first popularized in the management literature by Victor H. Vroom, *Work and Motivation* (New York: Wiley, 1964). Many textbooks now use the more user-friendly version of the theory introduced by Edward E. Lawler III, *Motivation in Work Organizations* (Monterey, CA: Brooks/Cole, 1973). Expectancy theory essentially predicts the motivation to engage in a behavior on the basis of the perceived probability (expectancy) that the behavior will lead to a given outcome, multiplied by the perceived value (valence) of that outcome. It is an adaptation of the expected value calculations familiar to economics.

4. Amatai Etzioni, *The Moral Dimension: Toward a New Economics* (New York: Free Press, 1988).

5. Abraham H. Maslow, *Motivation and Personality* (New York: Harper & Row, 1954); Edgar H. Schein, *Organizational Psychology* (Englewood Cliffs, NJ: Prentice-Hall, 1965).

6. This figure is adapted from figure 2 in Thomas and Jansen, "Intrinsic Motivation in the Military: Models and Strategic Importance," 16.

7. I am indebted to Bruce Vincent and Steve deBree of the New West Institute for coming up with the term "energy cycle" to describe this figure and for the phrase "energy leak."

8. A training and diagnostic tool, the *Work Engagement Profile* is a successor to the *Empowerment Inventory* described in the first edition of this book. The questions, which tap the four intrinsic rewards, are the same, but the interpretive materials have been updated to focus more directly on engagement and self-management and to provide descriptions of the experience of scoring high, medium, or low on each reward. The *Work Engagement Profile Technical Brief*, which describes the development, reliability, and validity of the instrument, is available online at http:// www.cpp.com.

9. More information about Professor Forest's study and findings is included in the *Work Engagement Profile Technical Brief*, which cites a technical brief he prepared for me on his findings. I am grateful to him for allowing me to cite his findings before he publishes them in the open literature.

10. This finding is also from Jacques Forest's study, as described in the *Work Engagement Profile Technical Brief*.

11. This finding was reported in Kenneth W. Thomas and Walter G. Tymon Jr., "Does Empowerment Always Work: Understanding the Role of Intrinsic Motivation and Personal Interpretation," *Journal of Management Systems* 6, no. 2 (1994): 1–13.

12. The finding on managerial innovativeness was reported by Gretchen Spreitzer in "Psychological Empowerment in the Workplace: Dimensions, Measurement, and Validation," *Academy of Management Journal* 38, no. 5 (1995): 1442–1465. Professor Teresa Amabile has done a great deal of research on the role of intrinsic motivation in work creativity and innovation. For two examples, see: T. M. Amabile, "Motivating Creativity in Organizations: On Doing What You Love and Loving What You Do," *California Management Review* 40, no. 1 (Fall 1997): 39–58; and R. Conti, T. M. Amabile, and S. Pollack, "Enhancing Intrinsic Motivation, Learning, and Creativity," *Personality and Social Psychology Bulletin* 21 (1995): 1107–1116.

13. This finding was reported in a study of project engineers by Steven Sutz, as cited in the *Work Engagement Profile Technical Brief*. It was also found in our large study of workers and managers in India, referred to later in this section, and also described in the *Work Engagement Profile Technical Brief*.

14. This finding has been reported in a number of studies, as cited in the *Technical Brief*.

15. For example, see the article by James L. Heskett, Thomas O. Jones, Gary W. Loveman, W. Earl Sasser Jr., and Leonard A. Schlesinger, "Putting the Service-Profit Chain to Work," *Harvard Business Review* 86, nos. 7–8 (2008): 118–129.

16. Some studies have measured commitment in terms of intent to remain. These are described in the following section on retention. The study reported here is from the India study, which measured commitment in broader terms involving loyalty and commitment.

17. Three studies on retention are described in more detail in the *Work Engagement Profile Technical Brief*.

18. The study of hospitality workers was reported by Raymond T. Sparrowe, "Empowerment in the Hospitality Industry: An Exploration of Antecedents and Outcomes," *Hospitality Research Journal* 17, no. 3 (1994): 51–73.

19. The study of reasons for remaining was by Jacques Forest, and is described in more detail in the *Technical Brief*.

20. The study on stress symptoms was reported by Thomas and Tymon, "Does Empowerment Always Work."

21. The study of hospitality workers is the previously cited one by Raymond Sparrowe, "Empowerment."

22. The project leader for this study was Richard Smith. Academic researchers included Professors Steven Stumpf, Walter Tymon, and Jonathan Doh from Villanova

University, and myself. The study was a partnership between Right Management, Inc., its Indian subsidiary India Grow Talent, and the academic research team. Preliminary results reported here are from data analyses run by Steven Stumpf. As of this writing, several papers are being prepared from this study.

Chapter 6

1. Thomas and Tymon, *Work Engagement Profile*.
2. Thomas and Tymon, *Work Engagement Profile*.
3. J. Richard Hackman, Greg Oldham, Robert Janson, and Kenneth Purdy, "A New Strategy for Job Enrichment," *California Management Review* 17, no. 4 (1975): 57–71; Hackman and Oldham, *Work Redesign*.
4. See the discussion of the role of interpretation in Thomas and Velthouse, "Cognitive Elements of Empowerment." That initial conceptual model identified individual differences in interpretive "styles" that were expected to influence intrinsic motivation. A later study by Thomas and Tymon, "Does Empowerment Always Work," identified a number of interpretive styles that influenced intrinsic motivation. Walt Tymon and I have continued to work with these interpretive styles and their effects, especially their contribution to stress. See Kenneth W. Thomas and Walter G. Tymon Jr., "Interpretive Styles That Contribute to Job-Related Stress: Two Studies of Managerial and Professional Employees," *Anxiety, Stress, and Coping* 8 (1995): 235–250; as well as a training instrument based upon this research, Kenneth W. Thomas and Walter G. Tymon Jr., *Stress Resiliency Profile* (Mountain View, CA: CPP, 1992). For a broad description of the role of managers' interpretive framing of events, see Bolman and Deal, *Reframing Organizations*.
5. As discussed in chapter 2, such leaders frame the purpose in terms that appeal to people's underlying values and create compelling visions of what it would be like to achieve that purpose. These are creative acts of interpretation that help people construct new meanings for a task purpose.
6. Charles C. Manz, *Mastering Self-Leadership* (Englewood Cliffs, NJ: Prentice-Hall, 1992).

Chapter 7

1. Thomas and Tymon, *Work Engagement Profile*.
2. Conversations with Bruce Vincent at the New West Institute and my wife and colleague, Gail Fann Thomas, have been particularly helpful.

Chapter 8

1. Oscar Wilde, *Lady Windermore's Fan,* act 3.
2. Thomas and Tymon, "Does Empowerment Always Work."
3. Thomas and Tymon, "Does Empowerment Always Work"; Thomas and Tymon, "Interpretive Styles That Contribute to Job-Related Stress," 235–250.
4. These recommendations are spelled out in greater detail in Thomas and Tymon, *Stress Resiliency Profile*.

5. Leider, *The Power of Purpose*, 25.
6. Leider, *The Power of Purpose*; Cliff Hakim, *We Are All Self-Employed* (San Francisco: Berrett-Koehler, 2003); Richard Nelson Bolles, *What Color Is Your Parachute? A Practical Manual for Job-Hunters and Career Changers* (Berkeley, CA: Ten Speed Press, 1999); Theresa M. Szczurek, *Pursuit of Passionate Purpose* (Hoboken, NJ: John Wiley & Sons, 2005).
7. Leider, *The Power of Purpose*, 70.
8. Peter Block, *The Empowered Manager* (San Francisco: Jossey-Bass, 1987), 102.
9. Leider, *The Power of Purpose*, 61, 119.
10. Hackman and Oldham, *Work Redesign*, 78.

Chapter 9
1. This quote is the title of a book on Jack Welch—Tichy and Sherman *Control Your Destiny or Someone Else Will: How Jack Welch Is Making General Electric the World's Most Competitive Corporation* (New York: Currency Doubleday, 1993).
2. Hakim, *We Are All Self-Employed*, 13.
3. Franklin Delano Roosevelt, First Inaugural Address, March 4, 1933.
4. Admiral William Rowley (then Captain Rowley), personal communication with the author, February 1993.
5. Max DePree, *Leadership Is an Art* (New York: Doubleday, 1989), 65.
6. Lawler, *From the Ground Up*, 31.

Chapter 10
1. Scott is the British novelist, author of *Ivanhoe*. Cited in Stuart Crainer, *The Ultimate Book of Business Quotations* (New York: Amacom, 1998), 95.
2. Abraham Maslow, "The Need to Know and the Fear of Knowing," *Journal of General Psychology* 68 (1963): 111–125.
3. Janelle Barlow and Claus Moller, *A Compliant Is a Gift: Using Customer Feedback as a Strategic Tool*, 1st ed. (San Francisco: Berrett-Koehler, 1996).
4. Sydney Finkelstein, *Why Smart Executives Fail: And What You Can Learn from Their Mistakes* (New York: Portfolio, 2003).
5. Rick Nelson, "Garden Party," 1972, MCA Records.
6. Mihaly Csikszentmihalyi, *Flow: The Psychology of Optimal Experience* (New York: Quality Paperback Book Club, Bookspan, 2001), 210.
7. From William Shakespeare, *Hamlet*, act 1, sc. 3.

Chapter 11
1. These are habits four through six in Stephen R. Covey, *The Seven Habits of Highly Effective People: Restoring the Character Ethic* (New York: Simon & Schuster, 1989).
2. This phrase was used in Dean G. Pruitt, "Strategic Choice in Negotiation," *American Behavioral Scientist* 27 (1983): 167–194; see also Dean G. Pruitt and Jeffrey Z. Rubin, *Social Conflict: Escalation, Stalemate, and Settlement* (New York: Random House, 1986).

3. Kenneth W. Thomas, *Introduction to Conflict Management* (Mountain View, CA: CPP, 2002), http://www.cpp.com.
4. Terrence E. Deal and M. K. Key, *Corporate Celebration* (San Francisco: Berrett-Koehler, 1998), 116.
5. Peters, *Thriving on Chaos,* 366.
6. Bob Nelson, *One Thousand and One Ways to Energize Employees* (New York: Workman, 1997), 66.
7. Nelson, *One Thousand and One Ways to Energize Employees*, 65.
8. Cited in Nelson, *One Thousand and One Ways to Energize Employees*, 90.

Chapter 12
1. I am indebted to Steve deBree and Bruce Vincent at the New West Institute for their comment that "this is what the conversation needs to be about" in a personal communication, 2008.
2. W. Edwards Deming used the term "intrinsic motivation" in his book *The New Economics for Industry, Government, Education* (Cambridge, MA: MIT Center for Advanced Engineering Study, 1993) and in his videotape series, *The Deming Library* (Chicago: Films Incorporated, 1991), vol. 15. He also used the term "joy in work" in *The New Economics*. He used the term "pride of workmanship" in his earlier book *Out of the Crisis* (Cambridge, MA: MIT Center for Advanced Engineering Study, 1986).
3. For more insights into credibility in leadership, see James M. Kouzes and Barry Z. Posner, *Credibility: How Leaders Gain and Lose It, Why People Demand It*, rev. ed. (San Francisco: Jossey-Bass, 2003).
4. I first interviewed then-Captain William Rowley in the early 1990s, before he was aware of my work. I was pleased that his points nevertheless fit into the four categories of my model. His leadership style and accomplishments at the naval hospital in Camp Pendleton were documented in M. B. Newton, "Effective Leadership through Empowerment: A Case Study," (master's thesis, Naval Postgraduate School, Monterey, CA, 1993). William Rowley is now a futurist at the Institute for Alternative Futures in Alexandria, Virginia.
5. For more on New West Institute, visit http://www.newwestinstitute.com. The three levels of engagement are described in Vincent, *The 3rd Way*.
6. This research finding was reported in Sparrowe, "Empowerment in the Hospitality Industry." His study is also described in the *Work Engagement Profile Technical Brief*.

Chapter 13
1. Thomas and Tymon, *Work Engagement Profile*. For more information, see the CPP Web site, http://www.cpp.com.
2. Professor Michael Frese, of the University of Giessen in Germany, has written extensively on the key role of initiative in today's work. For an example, see Frese and Fay, "Personal Initiative."

Chapter 14
1. Dean Kay and Kelly Grodon, "That's Life," performed by Frank Sinatra, Reprise Records, 1966.
2. Block, *Stewardship*, 221–231.
3. Block, *Stewardship*, 3.
4. This quote is from John Madden, *Hey, Wait a Minute* (New York: Ballantine-Fawcette, 1985) and was cited in Kouzes and Posner, *The Leadership Challenge,* 89.
5. Kouzes and Posner, *The Leadership Challenge*, 52.
6. Quoted in Noel Tichy and Ram Charan, "Speed, Simplicity, Self-Confidence: An Interview with Jack Welch," *Harvard Business Review* 67, no. 5 (September–October 1989): 119.
7. The G.E. Workout process has been widely described. See chapter 16 in Tichy and Sherman, *Control Your Destiny or Someone Else Will.*
8. Hackman and Oldham, *Work Redesign*, 78.

Chapter 15
1. For example, see Victor H. Vroom and Phillip W. Yetton, *Leadership and Decision-Making* (Pittsburgh: University of Pittsburgh Press, 1973). This model of leadership styles as decision methods is included in most management texts.
2. Edward E. Lawler III, *From the Ground Up: Six Principles for Building the New Logic Corporation* (San Francisco: Jossey-Bass, 1996), 31.
3. Thomas, Hocevar, and Thomas, "Operational, Tactical, and Strategic Meanings of Empowerment."
4. Collins and Porras, *Built to Last*, 152.
5. Steven Kerr (former chief learning officer, General Electric), personal communication with the author, 1993.
6. David McNally, *Even Eagles Need a Push* (New York: Doubleday, 1991).
7. This is "Point 8" in Deming, *Out of the Crisis.*
8. See chapter I-8, "Support Fast Failures," in Peters, *Thriving on Chaos,* 314–324.
9. The quote is from chapter 6 of *Alice in Wonderland*, reprinted in Lewis G. Carroll, *The Annotated Alice* (New York: Wings Books, 1998), 88.
10. Ken Blanchard, John P. Carlos, and Alan Randolph, *Empowerment Takes More Than a Minute,* 2nd ed. (San Francisco: Berrett-Koehler, 2001), 32.
11. Steven Kerr, personal communication with the author, 1993.

Chapter 16
1. Deming, *Out of the Crisis.*
2. Ashcroft is cited in Crainer, *The Ultimate Book of Business Quotations*, 221.
3. Deci, *Intrinsic Motivation*; Edward L. Deci and Richard M. Ryan, *Intrinsic Motivation and Self-Determination in Human Behavior* (New York: Plenum, 1985).
4. This term was coined by David L. Cooperrider. See Suresh Srivastva, David L. Cooperrider, and others, *Appreciative Management and Leadership: The Power of Positive Thought and Action in Organizations* (San Francisco: Jossey-Bass, 1990).
5. Deal and Key, *Corporate Celebration*, 47–48.

NOTES

6. Skill recognition was labeled an "interpretive style" and found to be related to a sense of competence in Thomas and Tymon, "Does Empowerment Always Work," 1–13. Low skill recognition was also found to predict stress in Thomas and Tymon, "Interpretive Styles That Contribute to Job-Related Stress," 235–250. Our measure is included in Thomas and Tymon, *Stress Resiliency Profile.*

7. Mihaly Csikszentmihalyi, *Finding Flow: The Psychology of Engagement in Everyday Life* (New York: Basic Books), 29–30.

8. Csikszentmihalyi, *Finding Flow*; Csikszentmihalyi, *Flow: The Psychology of Optimal Experience.*

9. Deming, *The New Economics for Industry, Government, Education*, 112.

10. Collins and Porras, *Built to Last*, 115–121.

Chapter 17

1. The original version of this model appeared in Kenneth W. Thomas, "Conflict and Conflict Management," in *Handbook of Industrial and Organizational Psychology*, ed. Marvin D. Dunnette (Chicago: Rand McNally, 1976) 889–935, which was written in 1971—five years before its publication. It was a refinement of ideas developed in Robert R. Blake and Jane S. Mouton, *The Managerial Grid* (Houston: Gulf, 1964). The model evolved with later theoretical developments. The version presented here is adapted from Kenneth W. Thomas and Ralph H. Kilmann, *Thomas-Kilmann Conflict Mode Instrument* (Mountain View, CA: CPP, 2002; originally published by Xicom, Inc., Tuxedo, NY, 1974).

2. For a more detailed account of the Camp David accords, see Shibley Telhami, *Power and Leadership in International Bargaining: The Path to the Camp David Accords* (New York: Columbia University Press, 1990).

3. For a diagnostic instrument that measures individuals' conflict-handling modes, see Thomas and Kilmann, *Thomas-Kilmann Conflict Mode Instrument.* This model is also explained and dramatized in a training video, *Dealing with Conflict* (Carlsbad, CA: CRM Films, 1992). For guidance on when and how to use each conflict-handling mode, see Thomas, *Introduction to Conflict Management.* For a practical guide to win–win negotiating, see Roger Fisher and William Ury, *Getting to Yes: Negotiating Agreement Without Giving In* (Boston: Houghton Mifflin, 1981).

4. D. Campbell, "If I'm in Charge, Why Is Everyone Laughing?" (Paper presented at the Center for Creative Leadership, Greensboro, NC, 1983.) Cited in Bolman and Deal, *Reframing Organizations*, 408.

5. Satchel (Leroy) Paige, from his 1953 book, *How to Keep Young.* Quoted in John Bartlett, *Familiar Quotations*, 15th ed. (Boston: Little, Brown, 1980), 867.

6. Deal and Key, *Corporate Celebration.*

7. Lawler, *From the Ground Up*, 29.

8. Lawler, *From the Ground Up*, 29.

9. Hackman and Oldham, *Work Redesign*, 137–138.

10. Peters, *Thriving on Chaos*, 330, 582.

Resource A

1. This section is based largely on the more detailed discussions in Kenneth W. Thomas and Walter G. Tymon Jr., "Bridging the Motivation Gap in Total Quality," *Quality Management Journal* 4, no. 2 (1997): 80–96, and in Thomas, Jansen, and Tymon, "Navigating in the Realm of Theory."

2. For a statement of the model and summary of initial research findings, see Deci, *Intrinsic Motivation.*

3. Deci and Ryan, *Intrinsic Motivation and Self-Determination in Human Behavior.*

4. Deci and Flaste, *Why We Do What We Do.*

5. This has been called the "overjustification effect." Later, more definitive studies of this issue have used meta-analysis techniques that combine the large number of individual studies that have been done on this issue and measure the significance of the effect for all the studies taken together. Two of these analyses have shown that the overjustification effect happens only under very constrained circumstances: J. Cameron and W. D. Pierce, "Reinforcement, Reward, and Intrinsic Motivation: A Meta-Analysis," *Review of Educational Research* 64, no. 3 (1994): 363–423, and U. J. Wiersma, "The Effects of Extrinsic Rewards in Intrinsic Motivation: A Meta-Analysis," *Journal of Occupational and Organizational Psychology* 65 (1992): 101–114. In organizational settings, extrinsic rewards tend to be positively related to reported intrinsic motivation.

6. Hackman, Oldham, Janson, and Purdy, "A New Strategy for Job Enrichment"; Hackman and Oldham, *Work Redesign.*

7. Herzberg's well-known model was published in Herzberg, Mausner, and Snyderman, *The Motivation to Work* (New York: Wiley, 1959). It lost credibility in the academic literature when empirical studies failed to support it. See Robert J. House and L. A. Wigdor, "Herzberg's Dual-Factor Theory of Job Satisfaction and Motivation: A Review of the Evidence and a Criticism," *Personnel Psychology* 20, no. 4 (1967): 369–389. Also see E. A. Locke, "Personnel Attitudes and Motivation," *Annual Review of Psychology* 26 (1975): 457–480.

8. See the relevant portions of these two reviews of research results on the Hackman-Oldham model: Y. Fried and G. R. Ferris, "The Validity of the Job Characteristics Model: A Review and Meta-Analysis," *Personnel Psychology* 40, no. 2 (1987): 287–322; and R. W. Renn and R. J. Vandenberg, "The Critical Psychological States: An Underrepresented Component in Job Characteristics Model Research," *Journal of Management* 21, no. 2 (1995): 279–303.

Resource B

1. John R. Deckop, Robert Mangel, and Carol C. Cirka, "Getting More Than You Pay For: Organizational Citizenship Behavior and Pay-for-Performance Plans," *Academy of Management Journal* 42, no. 4 (1999): 420–428.

INDEX

ABOUT THE AUTHOR

Ken Thomas has made a career of finding meaningful challenges that face managers in organizations and then providing new solutions for dealing with them. His work combines highly respected academic research with practical training and consulting. His earliest work was in conflict management, where he developed an international reputation for his research and for his training materials. The *Thomas-Kilmann Conflict Mode Instrument,* which he designed with Ralph Kilmann, has sold over six million copies and is translated into several languages.

For some time now, Ken's other interest has been the intrinsic rewards that power employee engagement and empowerment. He has conducted interviews and surveys of leaders and followers in many organizations, written influential academic articles on intrinsic motivation, developed the *Work Engagement Profile* with Walter Tymon, conducted training workshops, provided consulting to both public- and private-sector organizations, delivered presentations to professional organizations, and worked closely with other consultants and trainers on this topic. Most recently, he participated in a large-scale study of intrinsic motivation in twenty-eight companies in India.

Academically, Ken has been a professor of management at UCLA, Temple University, the University of Pittsburgh, where he was also director of the PhD program, and the Naval Postgraduate School in Monterey, California. He holds a PhD from Purdue University in administrative sciences.

Ken lives with his wife, Gail Fann Thomas, in Monterey. He enjoys hiking along the Big Sur coastline.

Ken is available for presentations and workshops and would also like to hear of your experiences applying the ideas in this book. Ken can be contacted via his Web site: http://www .kennethwthomas.net.

THE ASTD MISSION:

Through exceptional learning and performance, we create a world that works better.

The American Society for Training & Development provides world-class professional development opportunities, content, networking, and resources for workplace learning and performance professionals.

Dedicated to helping members increase their relevance, enhance their skills, and align learning to business results, ASTD sets the standard for best practices within the profession.

The society is recognized for shaping global discussions on workforce development and providing the tools to demonstrate the impact of learning on the organizational bottom line. ASTD represents the profession's interests to corporate executives, policy makers, academic leaders, small business owners, and consultants through world-class content, convening opportunities, professional development, and awards and recognition.

Resources
- T+D (Training + Development) Magazine
- ASTD Press
- Industry Newsletters
- Research and Benchmarking
- Representation to Policy Makers

Networking
- Local Chapters
- Online Communities
- ASTD Connect
- Benchmarking Forum
- Learning Executives Network

Professional Development
- Certificate Programs
- Conferences and Workshops
- Online Learning
- CPLP™ Certification Through the ASTD Certification Institute
- Career Center and Job Bank

Awards and Best Practices
- ASTD BEST Awards
- Excellence in Practice Awards
- E-Learning Courseware Certification (ECC) Through the ASTD Certification Institute

Learn more about ASTD at www.astd.org.
1.800.628.2783 (U.S.) or 1.703.683.8100
customercare@astd.org

ABOUT BERRETT-KOEHLER PUBLISHERS

Berrett-Koehler is an independent publisher dedicated to an ambitious mission: **Creating a World That Works for All.**

We believe that to truly create a better world, action is needed at all levels—individual, organizational, and societal. At the individual level, our publications help people align their lives with their values and with their aspirations for a better world. At the organizational level, our publications promote progressive leadership and management practices, socially responsible approaches to business, and humane and effective organizations. At the societal level, our publications advance social and economic justice, shared prosperity, sustainability, and new solutions to national and global issues.

A major theme of our publications is "Opening Up New Space." They challenge conventional thinking, introduce new ideas, and foster positive change. Their common quest is changing the underlying beliefs, mindsets, institutions, and structures that keep generating the same cycles of problems, no matter who our leaders are or what improvement programs we adopt.

We strive to practice what we preach—to operate our publishing company in line with the ideas in our books. At the core of our approach is stewardship, which we define as a deep sense of responsibility to administer the company for the benefit of all of our "stakeholder" groups: authors, customers, employees, investors, service providers, and the communities and environment around us.

We are grateful to the thousands of readers, authors, and other friends of the company who consider themselves to be part of the "BK Community." We hope that you, too, will join us in our mission.

BE CONNECTED

Visit Our Website

Go to www.bkconnection.com to read exclusive previews and excerpts of new books, find detailed information on all Berrett-Koehler titles and authors, browse subject-area libraries of books, and get special discounts.

Subscribe to Our Free E-Newsletter

Be the first to hear about new publications, special discount offers, exclusive articles, news about bestsellers, and more! Get on the list for our free e-newsletter by going to www .bkconnection.com.

Get Quantity Discounts

Berrett-Koehler books are available at quantity discounts for orders of ten or more copies. Please call us toll-free at (800) 929-2929 or email us at bkp.orders@aidcvt.com.

Host a Reading Group

For tips on how to form and carry on a book reading group in your workplace or community, see our website at www .bkconnection.com.

Join the BK Community

Thousands of readers of our books have become part of the "BK Community" by participating in events featuring our authors, reviewing draft manuscripts of forthcoming books, spreading the word about their favorite books, and supporting our publishing program in other ways. If you would like to join the BK Community, please contact us at bkcommunity@ bkpub.com.